To Olive

with best wishes

Sid Sheppy

THORNGUMBALD

That Village Yon Side of Hedon

G. S. Skeggs

'The moving finger writes, and, having writ,
Moves on; nor all thy piety nor wit
Shall lure it back to cancel half a line,
Nor all thy tears wash out a word of it.'
Rubáiyát of Omar Khayyám

Highgate Publications (Beverley) Limited
1990

ACKNOWLEDGEMENTS

I would like to thank the following for their help during the production of this book:

Mrs. Deirdre Alcock, who was responsible for the majority of the typing of the original manuscript and corrected many of the initial errors; Mrs. Sheila Gardner, who passed on information she unearthed in the course of her own local history researches on Thorngumbald; D.I.A. Ltd. of Hedon, who helped with the reproduction of maps and photocopying; and Willinghams of Thorngumbald who have helped in many ways.

Many other people have assisted me during the compilation of this book, particularly people in the village. There are, unfortunately, too many to mention individually and I hope they will accept this as my collective thanks to them all.

My thanks also go to the staff of the following for their help in the collection of source material:

Beverley Reference Library; Borthwick Institute of Historical Research (York); Brynmor Jones Library, University of Hull; Hedon Library; Hull Local Studies Library; Humberside County Record Office (Beverley).

I express my appreciation of Willinghams of Thorngumbald who have assisted publication of this book with financial sponsorship.

All the author's profits from the book are being donated to village causes and organisations.

British Library Cataloguing in Publication Data

Skeggs, G. S. (George Sidney)
 Thorngumbald: that village yon side of Hedon.
 1. Humberside, history
 I. 942.83

ISBN 0-948929-35-9   © G. S. Skeggs 1990

Published by Highgate Publications (Beverley) Ltd.
24 Wylies Road, Beverley, HU17 7AP
Telephone (0482) 866826

Printed and Typeset in 10 on 11pt Plantin by
B.A. Press, 2-4 Newbegin, Lairgate, Beverley, HU17 8EG
Telephone (0482) 882232

Cover: 'Fodlass' Well (probably a corruption of 'Furdales'), filled in during the 1960s.

THORNGUMBALD
THAT VILLAGE YON SIDE OF HEDON

When we village residents are asked where we live, and reply, 'Thorngumbald', if the questioner is local, the next comment tends to be, 'Oh, yes, I know that village, just yon side of Hedon.' Strangers, however, usually have a look of blank amazement on their faces, and reply, 'Thorn *what?*' and we end up having to spell it out. Another unusual feature of the name is that, in an area noted for its dropping of letters and shortening of names, many locals manage to add an 'in' to the name, making it Thorn*in*gumbald; the same fate is given to another local place, Withernsea, credited with an extra 'en' and becoming Wither*en*sea.

So where did this strange name of Thorngumbald come from? The popular belief in this area is that it arose from 'Thorn cum Paull', an idea probably derived from trade directories produced in the early 1800s which gave this derivation of the name. The error was compounded by later directories which, even into this century, were still giving the same origin of the name. This misconception is understandable, because the church at Thorngumbald was, until recent times, always attached to the mother church at Paull. However, the assumption was incorrect, as a look at the history of the village shows.

The first mention of the village name is in Domesday Book (1086) when it is given as 'Torn', an old English word meaning 'thorn bush'. This name was still in use in 1228, but by 1260 had acquired an 'h' and 'e' to become 'Thorne'. In the Lay Subsidy Rolls of Edward I (1297) it is given as 'Thorengumbaud', Gumbaud being the family name of the then Lord of the Manor, an old French personal name which itself is derived from the old German name, 'Gundabald'. The village received many different spellings up to the 17th century: *Thorngumbaud, Thorngumbold, Thorneygumbald, Gumberthorn* being just some examples. The present spelling appears to be the one in use since then.

Other areas of the parish are also mentioned from very early times, Stockholm Farm is now on the area called Stockholmlands in the 10th and 11th centuries and later called Stockholmlandes. Far Marsh was Outmarsh in 1579. At the same time Greenmarsh was Greenmarshe and in 1615 was Thorngreenmarsh. An area called Le Rigge in 1339 was still known as Riggs until recent times. Other areas were Le Summergangs (Summergangs) in 1605 and Thornyngcrofte (Thorneycroft) in 1301. Some of our street names are based on these ancient areas of the parish, but I am pleased the planners did not use all the old names — 'Far Five Stengs Drive' and 'Mean Gordales Road' would not be very popular with residents!

So much for the name. What of the village itself? Today we see a busy modern commuter village on the main road to Withernsea and south-east

Holderness. In fact, it has the largest village population in Holderness — over 3,000. This all began with the building expansion of the 1960s and 70s when Thorngumbald was turned from a quiet, sleepy village of under 300 people to the present size. But what of its past? How did it evolve into the village as we see it now? To find any documented evidence of the village or the whole area of Holderness before Domesday Book is very difficult. What survives is archaeological evidence from the Ice Age. As the great sheets melted and receded, the whole of Holderness became a vast deposit of the great northern drift, the natural drainage of the area being to the Humber, rather than the sea. This drainage being poor, it left great areas of water penned up, which formed into a series of lakes and marshy areas which could be likened to the Norfolk Broads or fenlands. These areas were inhabited by a race of lake-dwelling people, and it is probable that the very earliest inhabitants of Thorngumbald were this type of people.

The next group of whom we have knowledge are a tribe called the Parisii, a pastoral people, farmers and herdsmen, who inhabited the East Riding up to Roman times. Although there is no evidence of their occupation, it is probable that, as the drainage of the area slowly improved, they inhabited the high ground and became our first farmers.

There are no signs of any Roman influence on Thorngumbald, but, when they withdrew in c.410, they left a vacuum in the country, and the unprotected inhabitants were open to attack from all kinds of marauding bands. To protect themselves against such attacks the British sought the assistance of a group of Saxon sea pirates who, after driving out the invaders, promptly subjugated the Britons. The Angles in particular settled in Holderness — Ottringham, Keyingham and Thorngumbald, 'Torne' as it was then, are all Anglian place names.

When the Angles settled in the area they made many changes which still affect us today; one which had great impact was the introduction of the maulboard plough drawn by a team of eight oxen, a much more efficient implement than the one used by the ancient Britons, enabling the fertile clays to be cultivated more easily. This plough also determined the field patterns; the small Celtic field changed to the large open field system that endured until 1757 in Thorngumbald. It is possible that at this time Thorngumbald was actually on the banks of the Humber, like Ottringham and Keyingham; there is much evidence to show that the banks were then much further inland than today.

The next group of people to leave their mark on the area were the Vikings, Norsemen, or Northmen, as they were called; they started raiding and plundering Britain in c.793, and by 874 Halfdene the Dane had Yorkshire settled on him, divided into the present Ridings.

A feature of the East Riding is that it was split into 'Hundreds', rather than Wapentakes, by the Danes, an unusual feature in the North; in fact no other shire north of Leicestershire has this feature, except for small parts of

Lancashire and Cheshire. The Holderness Hundreds were North, Middle and South, Thorngumbald being in the South Hundred. The South Hundred was all land south of the line from below Tunstall and Burstwick, excluding Hedon, which did not exist at this time and was created from parts of Preston and Burstwick in the 12th century.

The name, Holderness, is of Danish origin and is derived from the word 'Holder', an officer of high rank, and 'Ness', a promontory or headland, but there are, in fact, very few place names of Danish origin in Holderness. The influence of the Danes in this area is written on every page of Domesday Book. Villeins and Sokemen were their terms for the farmers and peasants, and the system of measurement of land they brought was different. Instead of the English hide, divided into virgates, we have the carucate divided into oxgangs, the whole system of calculation being different. The hide was the amount of land necessary to maintain a family. The carucate was the amount of land a plough could cultivate in two years, assuming a two-field system (one field left fallow each year). This was general in the area. The carucate was divided into eight oxgangs, depending on how many oxen were drawing the plough. The term, oxgang, was still in use locally until recent times.

Domesday Book also lists the last owners of the land before the Norman Conquest. It states that in the time of Edward the Confessor Thorngumbald belonged to the Manor of Burstwick, which was held by Earl Tostig, the brother of the eventual King Harold. After Harold defeated Tostig at Stamford Bridge it passed to Earl Morcar.

Thorngumbald — a quiet rural scene in the 1930s.

[Reproduced by kind permission of Martin Craven]

The South Holderness marshlands in 1660

[*Reproduced from June A. Sheppard's The Draining of the Marshlands of South Holderness and the Vale of York by kind permission of the East Yorkshire Local History Society.*]

NORTH SEA

SPURN HEAD

KILNSEA FLEET

EASINGTON FLEET

WINESTEAD FLEET

OLD HEAD SAND

NORTH CHANNEL

KEYINGHAM FLEET

SUNK SAND

HEDON FLEET

HEART CORE SAND

OLD FLEET

RIVER HUMBER MAIN CHANNEL

RIVER HULL

SAND BANKS

EDGE OF HIGH GROUND

POSSIBLE MEDIEVAL COASTLINE

Miles
0 1 2 3

THE NORMANS

The Norman invasion of 1066 and King Harold's defeat at Hastings were the beginning of a new era in Holderness and of the first documented evidence that we have of Thorngumbald.

We know that William the Conqueror gave Holderness to a Fleming called Drogo de la Beuvrière who, as well as coming to England with the Conqueror, was married to one of his relatives. The story is that he accidentally killed his wife, Albina, and, fearing William's wrath, fled the country and was never heard of again. The only thing that Drogo appears to have done of interest was that he was probably the builder of the castle at Skipsea. When he was actually given Holderness is not certain. He definitely held it in 1086, as Domesday Book confirms.

After the disappearance of Drogo, William granted Holderness to Odo, the dispossessed Count of Champagne who was also Count of Aumale, a small county in north-eastern Normandy. He had received Aumale when he married William the Conqueror's sister, Adelaide, who had inherited it from her first husband. Odo was dispossessed of Holderness in 1096 after being involved in a plot to overthrow the King, and it passed for a short time to Arnulf De Montgomery, before passing to Odo's son, Stephen, about 1102.

The next Lord of Holderness was Stephen's son, William, who was known as Le Gros from his size; he probably took the title about 1130. William Le Gros is probably the best known of the Lords of Holderness, and was featured in many Yorkshire chronicles. In a battle near Northallerton, against King David of the Scots, William was mentioned as the English commander. He may have been an excellent commander, but it would appear his personal combat prowess could not have been very high as by 1150 it was reported that he was so fat he could no longer ride a horse! In fact it was probably this which led to the founding of the first monastery in Holderness at Meaux. The story is that William had made a vow to go to Jerusalem, which, because of his age and weight, he was unable to fulfil; however, a monk from Fountains Abbey, named Adam, promised him absolution if he founded another Cistercian abbey. Adam chose Meaux for his site, an area already procured to make a park. This led to the Cistercian dominance of Holderness that followed. William died in 1179 and was succeeded by his legitimate daughter, Hawisa.

Hawisa was now Countess of Aumale in her own right and one of England's more desirable heiresses, having Holderness and lands in Lincolnshire and south-east England, the Barony of Copeland, and the Honour of Skipton. Her first husband was William De Mandeville, Earl of Essex, who was frequently out of England on royal business and who also completed two crusades; he died in 1189. King Richard then arranged for her to marry William De Forz I, an act she at first resisted. Luckily he appears to have spent most of the period of their marriage on the crusades, dying in 1195.

Her third husband was Baldwin De Bethune whom she married in 1195. Baldwin was a Flemish knight who accompanied Richard on his crusade in 1192; they were captured on their way home in 1194 and he was held hostage in Vienna for the King. He died at Burstwick in 1212 where he had probably built the manor house, as by this time they had moved from Skipsea.

The next lord, William De Forz II, Hawisa's son by William De Forz I, was completely domiciled in England and was, it seems, a very unpredictable man who during his life time changed sides both for and against the King. He also appears to have not been very astute with his money, as, at his death in 1241 on his way to the crusade, he left many debts to his son and heir, William De Forze III, probably the least interesting of the Lords of Holderness.

As he left no heir to Holderness, various claimants came forward, but in the end it was awarded to John De Eston who claimed he was descended from a daughter of William Le Gros. He immediately surrendered it to the King and thus it marked the end of the Lords of Holderness, as it remained a Crown estate until the end of the Middle Ages, finally passing to the Constable family of Burton Constable in 1557.

Norman font in St. Mary's Church.

[Martyn Kirby]

MANOR HOUSES

Manor houses in Thorngumbald existed into the Middle Ages on the estates of three families, the Newmarkets, Tyrwhits, and Holmes. We know that two of them existed in the 1900s, although the Holme family manor house is, strictly speaking, at Paull Holme, where a surviving tower is still to be seen just off the road to Paull. This tower is part of the north wing of what appears to have been a manor built in the form of a letter H dating from the 14th century and probably rebuilt c.1715. The other manor house, which existed until the 1960s and was then called Manor Farm, was built in the 19th century, but it is said an earlier manor house stood to the west of its site. In fact, it is recorded that the previous manor house had 'weathered the storms of four centuries', so dating it to the 15th century. In his *History of Holderness*, Poulson states that 'the common pound has always stood on the land of that particular family and is perhaps the only sign of Manorial Authority'. The site of the third manor house has never been identified but would almost certainly have been on the south side of the Main Road, as until the 1700s all buildings appear to have been arranged along this side, possibly because, before the Enclosure Act of 1757, the common fields stretched along the north side of the Main Road.

Amenity Area: site of former Manor Houses and later Manor Farm.   *[Martyn Kirby]*

THE LORDS OF THE MANOR

As mentioned previously, Thorngumbald was part of the Manor of Burstwick at the time of the Conquest and belonged to Earl Morcar, who had earlier helped defeat Tostig, the previous owner, on behalf of King Harold (Earl Morcar held Kilnsea Manor and other properties before the Conquest).

Domesday Book states that 'Drogo De Beuvrière holds Burstwick and to this Manor belongs the soc of Torn with two carucates of land'. By 1280, Drogo had sub-infuedated [granted to a subordinate] this land to Galfrid De Gumbaud.

This is the first mention of the Gumbaud family, and we must assume that between 1086 and this time the Saxon landowner of Thorngumbald had lost his lands and this Flemish knight had been installed; whether the Gumbauds had beeen knights in William the Conqueror's army, or had been in the service of one of the Counts of Aumale, is unclear; my belief is that they probably came over with Baldwin De Bethune who became the second husband of Hawisa, Countess of Aumale, in 1195. In Kirby's *Inquest*, 5 March 1281, Galfrid Gumbaud is recorded as holding two carucates of land in Thorngumbald, but by 1291 his son William had succeeded to the manor. In 1303 the same William was granted the rights of 'free warren' (that is such things as hunting and fishing). William Gumbaud died in 1305 and the manor was beqeathed to his sisters who were: Laura, wife of David of Flitwick; Margaret, wife of Laurence of Holbeach; Christine, a nun at Stirkwald, Lincolnshire, and Joan, a nun at Swine Priory. Laura evidently married again, because in 1316 the Sheriff's Return of the names and possessors of Holderness villages shows the Manor of Thorngumbald as held by Thomas Newmarket, husband of Laura, Laurence of Holbeach, and Edmund Wastney, husband of Christine, who must have given up the cloth and married. From this time onwards, the Manor of Thorngumbald never belonged to a single person. Thereafter the land was divided and subdivided among many families in a complex series of transactions. [See Appendix for explanatory diagram.]

Land eventually passed into the Cheyney family when Anne, the daughter of John Holme, married William Cheyney; it then passed to his son, William. It is probably this William who is mentioned in Glover's *Visitation* of 1585 as one of the 'Gentlemen of Holderness'; his address was given as Burstall Garth (Burstall is one of the lost villages of East Yorkshire, now in the Humber near Skeffling). He is also mentioned again in 1584 when a muster of horsemen was ordered at Tollerton Plain before the Lord Lieutenant of the County on 27 March; among the Holderness contingent was William Cheyney with one horse (some had two!). William died in 1599 and was succeeded by his son, Christopher, who was also mentioned as

8

resident at Thorngumbald and Burstall Garth. He in turn left it to his three daughters: Anne, who was married to John Duncalfe, Elizabeth, who was married to Captain John Turner, and Jane, who was married to John Faucett (or Fawsitt). It was the Fawsitt share which eventually passed to Sarah Mauleverer who owned the Manor (Manor Farm) in 1810, and her heirs sold it in several lots in 1854.

Another Manor in Thorngumbald was held in 1370 by Sir William Goodrich. It was held by a family called Tyrwhit from the 15th century and was sold by Robert Tyrwhit in 1598 to Roger and Robert Anderson. At the time of the Enclosures in 1757 it was held by the Gee family of Bishop Burton. In 1766 it was sold to William Scott, who in turn sold it to James Kay in 1793, Samuel Standidge buying it from him in 1796. After this, the Manor of Thorngumbald ceased to exist as such; in fact, as one can see from later transactions, changes in society had brought about more frequent selling of land.

'Fodlass' Well (probably a corruption of 'Furdales'), filled in during the 1960s.

St. Mary's Church with the tower which was removed in 1855.

St. Mary's Church, 1990.

RELIGION AND THE CHURCH

The first mention of Christianity in Thorngumbald is in the 12th century, when it was recorded that Stephen, Earl of Albemarle and Lord of Holderness, granted the revenue of Torne to the Benedictine Abbey at St. Martin D'Auchy on the east bank of the river Bressle in Normandy, the Diocese of Rouen. This is the first mention of the church, or chapel as it was called for most of its years, and it is generally thought that it was in existence by 1115 when the mother church at Paull and the nearby church at Burstwick were given to Aumale Abbey.

In Domesday Book approximately 60 places in the East Riding with priests were recorded, a curious fact in view of the almost complete absence of Anglo-Saxon churches in the area today. Over the centuries many churches have been pulled down and re-built, and all traces of earlier building work lost, but, even so, if we compare the paucity of the Norman churches in Holderness with Lincolnshire, a similar area with a large number of Anglo-Saxon churches, this is puzzling.

It is hard to believe that the 'Harrying of the North' could be responsible for the wholesale destruction of Holderness churches, for there is no evidence that this area suffered badly in this respect: In fact, we appear to have suffered little of the devastation that other areas of Yorkshire endured. A more likely explanation is that Holderness is an area devoid of building stone and, rather than incur the heavy costs of transporting the stone from afar, the buildings were of wooden construction until Norman times.

The church of Thorngumbald was superintended in England by Burstall Priory, near Skeffling, a cell of Aumale Abbey, and was probably served by itinerant monks from there, rather than having its own priest. The monks would collect the revenue which at the time would be considerable, and forward proceeds to the Abbey in Normandy. In the late 12th century the duty of collection and half the endowment were transferred to a local vicar.

Aumale Abbey still held the chapel at Thorngumbald in 1295, but their property was seized by the King of France during the French wars and this must have prompted Aumale Abbey to sell it in 1396 to Kirkstall Abbey. At that time it contained a chantry endowed with the house and garth of its chaplain. The chapel evidently became disused and at the suppression of the chantry in 1589 the chapel was described as 'decayed and late belonging to Kirkstall Abbey'.

This period of decline co-incided with the reign of Henry VIII (1509-1547) who, notorious for his many wives, was responsible for a much more far-reaching act, when in 1534 he broke with the Pope over his matrimonial problems and declared himself head of the Church of England. He closed monasteries (including Kirkstall Abbey) and sold off their property.

In 1547 Henry was succeeded by the boy King Edward VI and in his reign

Blocked Norman arch on south side of the church. [Martyn Kirby]

Hatchment with monogram of Queen Victoria but depicting coat of arms of George I.

[Martin Kirby]

12

the Reformation was taken a step further by the abolishing of the mass. In 1547 the chantries were suppressed and their lands and revenues appropriated, and in 1549 an English prayer book was issued for compulsory use. The chantry at Thorngumbald chapel would be one of these and no further mention is made of it.

At the time of the Reformation the church lost much of its wealth. For example, Ralph Rokesby, who died in 1525, left land and houses at Thorngumbald to his nephews, John and Nicholas, to support a chantry in St. Mary's Church, Sandal, West Yorkshire. In 1535 these properties were worth £5 per year. Their loss was most likely one of the major causes of the decline of the fabric of the church.

In 1558 the mother church at Paull, and presumably Thorngumbald also, was granted to Nicholas, Archbishop of York. It is, however, doubtful if the Archbishop took up this grant, as in 1564 the Crown held both churches. In 1589 the chapel of Thorngumbald was granted to Sir Edward Stanley; by 1633 it belonged to Thomas Cheyney. In the 1590s the inhabitants of Thorngumbald had obtained the use of the chapel as well as certain parochial rights (including the solemnisation of marriages) and by the 17th century baptisms also took place there. In 1650 it was recommended that the chapel be made a parish church for Thorngumbald and Camerton. These rights were lost some time later, but the churchyard was consecrated in 1896 and the chapel was licensed again for marriages in 1942.

In 1954 the church was removed from its annexation with Paull and was joined with the Church at Burstwick, but in 1988 became a parish church in its own right, being severed from its connection with the church at Burstwick.

The original Norman church has seen many changes in its construction. The blocked doorway on the south side of the church still retains its Norman arch and is probably in its original position, while the smaller door at the entrance to the vestry with its engrailed moulding is also probably 12th-century but appears to have been re-sited there some time in the past. The font at the west end is also of this period and, although plain, is nevertheless beautiful in its simplicity. The existing windows are 15th-century and there is a section of a jamb of a chancel arch set in the east wall, also probably from the same date.

In 1715 the chancel was said to be in disrepair. The tower of the church was built in brick in 1768, and other restoration was undertaken at this time, including the installation of pews to accommodate 100 people. Since that date, the pews on the south side have had to be shortened, probably to allow easier access for bridal processions, the original width being insufficient.

A pulpit was fixed to the south wall near to the vestry door and a vestry, built of local handmade brick, was added at the same time. The west gallery was removed but there are still remains of wooden beams set in the top of the west wall, probably the supports of this gallery. The cost of this work was

£60, towards which Captain Samuel Standidge contributed £30 and the village the other £30.

The tower was removed in 1858 when the church was again restored and the present bellcote supported by two buttresses was built containing one bell (there had been a bell in the church in 1552). The pulpit was removed to the north side of the chancel and the building re-roofed. All this left the church looking much as we see it today. The building itself is a mixture of brick and rubble, with ashlar dressing, indication of the many alterations and repairs that have been carried out over the years.

It is known that the church grounds were enclosed until 1840 and no burials took place until 1897. However, when the churchyard was reducecd in c.1790, and excavation took place on the south side, many human bones were found, evidence of its use for common burials at a much earlier date. The present cemetery on the north side of the Main Road at the western end of the village was opened in 1937 and is still in use. A humorist once remarked: 'The people in Thorngumbald were so healthy they had to shoot someone to start it off!

Although the church at Thorngumbald is not an example of rich architecture, it nevertheless has some beautifully simple Communion vessels. One large pewter flagon is a fine example of early craftsmanship and two pewter alms dishes of about 10″ diameter still show an intricate cross-lined pattern in the centre and a worked outer section: these date from the Reformation at the latest and may even be earlier. They may be items bought with money left in wills: the will of Thomas Sheys, dated October, 1446, gave to the altar of St. Mary's 3s 4d for ornaments for the altar chapel, while the will of John Garton of Hull, dated 17 March, 1455, gave £5 for the same purpose. Five pounds was a considerable sum of money and would most probably have been sufficient to buy these items. Another worthy possession is a silver chalice and cover, hallmarked HULL 1706, bearing the following inscription: 'This plate belongs to Thorngumbald Chapel, Robert Bucker, John Cookman, Churchwardens 1712'. I have not been able to identify the donor of this chalice.

Other Points of Interest in the Church

Alms Box. Just inside the main north entrance to the church is a mediaeval alms box mounted on a wooden pedestal, originally provided for the relief of the poor.

Organ. In the north-west corner of the church stands this magnificent small chamber organ, built by Lincoln & Son of London and thought to date from c.1810. Although a considerable sum of money is needed to bring it into first-class working order, it still remains a superb example of this type of organ.

'Victorian' Hatchment. This is on the north wall near the entrance door.

During recent refurbishment and cleaning it was discovered that the coat of arms depicted on it dates from the time of George I, indicating that it was probably installed during the last refurbishment of the church before 1858.

Thorngumbald must have been quite a well-behaved village as, in a Tudor Visitation Book of 1595/6, no complaints or defects are recorded there. It makes interesting reading and I have reproduced below the section including Thorngumbald:

Beforde Nil

Marflete (blank)	Mr. Seale there parson is not residente nor kepes
Siglesthorne	hospitalitie. He haithe 2 benefices Siglesthorne and Bolton juxta Bollande. One of the syde iles is in decay in defalte ether of Mr. Archedeacon Remyngton or Mr. Hillarie Daykins.
	Tho. Robinson now of Bransburton and laite of Catfosse refusethe to pay his cesmente to the repaire of the churche and other necessarie uses of the parishe being xxiiid [23 pence].
Thorngumbalde	Nil.
Hilston	The chancell windowes ar in decay in defalt of Mr. John Dringe there parson.
	Henrie Segs, Robte Barret and Willm. Meedlay for brawlinge in the churche yarde. This Segs was the begyner of bothe the quarels.
Drypoole	Anne Harrison wife of Ricd Harrison and Agnes Atkinson scoulded in the churche yarde to the offence of the congregacion.
Bransburton	2 fornicators.
Hesell	5 fornicators and 3 scolds.
Patrington	Mr. Humphrey Hall parson dothe use huntinge in the feelde dyvers tymes. 20 July 1596 Mr. Jo Benet LL.D. iniunxit eidem Mr. Hall not to frequent huntinge offensively sub pena juris.

Although the church at Thorngumbald was attached to the church at Paull, a house belonged to it in Thorngumbald and the Vicar of Paull lived there in the 16th century. This half-acre of land is possibly that which was bought by the Parish Council in 1936 for the sum of £112. 10s. (Chairman Mr. John S. Andrews and Messrs L. Crossley and Wm. Cockerill) and became the present cemetery.

There was also a chaplain of Thorngumbald in the 15th century, and an assistant curate was said to have been obtained by the inhabitants and supported by tythes in the 16th century.

Probably the best known local personality to have ties with the church is John Tickell who published the well-known *History of Hull* in 1798. Tickell, who was the curate of Preston with Hedon, and actually lived in Fletchergate, Hedon, regularly signed the Thorngumbald register from 1783 to 1794. There is also a payment of £10 made to him in the Paull tythe book of 1794.

In 1743 Archbishop Herring of York sent to each church a paper of questions which became known as Archbishop Herring's Visitation Returns. The return for Thorngumbald is given below:

I. There are Twenty One Familys [sic] within the Chappelry of Thorn Gumbald & not one Dissenter of any Sort among them. There are also three Families at a Place call'd Cammerton within the Chappelry; which makes in all Twenty Four

II. There is is [sic] no Meeting House of any Sort within the Chappelry

III. There is no Charity School within the Chappelry but there is a School taught by one John Holmes who teaches about Twenty Five Children to read English & Write & instructs them in the Church Catechism, & takes care to bring them to Church.

IV. There is an Alms-House Maintaind by the Inhabitants of the Chappelry, where in Two Poor People dwell, who are Maintained by the rest of the Inhabitants.

V. I do not reside in the House belonging to the Chappelry but in the Vicarage House of the Parish of Skeckling with Burstwick

VI. I have no Curate.

VII. I know of none who come to Church in the Chapelry that are not Baptized, or that being Baptized, & of a Competent Age, are not confirm'd except those who come this Day in order to be confirmd

VIII. The publick Service is read in the Chapel on every other Sunday betwixt Lady Day & Michaelmas, & on Every Third Sunday betwixt Michaelmas & Lady Day beginning about one of the clock in the Afternoon except on Such Days as the Sacrament is Administred [sic] and then it is performd in the forenoon

IX. I do not Catechise in the Chapel at any time except against a Confirmation but I order the Children & Servants to come to the Mother-Church of Paul [sic] to be instructed in the Catechism, whither some of them do come.

X. The Sacrament of the Lords Supper is administred in the Chapel Four times in the Year, & I believe about Thirty persons or better do communicate at other times & there were Six or Seven & Thirty at Easter last

XI. I do give open & timely warning of the Sacrament before it is administred. My Parishioners do not send in their names beforehand. I have not refused the Sacrament to any one.

Will. Robson   Curate of Thorn Gumbald.

By 1836 there was a weekly service with Communion celebrated four or six times a year. By 1894 this was weekly.

In 1851, in addition to the normal public census that was conducted, there was a religious census, with the clergy counting their congregations one Sunday. Thorngumbald's entry is as follows:

Thorngumbald Chapel of Ease (St. Mary's)

WHEN CONSECRATED — perhaps nearly 1,000 yrs. ago.

UNDER WHAT CIRCUMSTANCES — no one can tell on account of its great antiquity.

HOW OR BY WHOM ERECTED — not known

HOW ENDOWED — gratis by the Vicar with many thanks? *[sic]*

SPACES FOR SITTING — free sitting — 20
other sitting 40. Total — 60.

GENERAL CONGREGATION MORNING — 42.

REMARKS. In the Summer there may be 50 persons as a congregation and 10 or 12 Sunday Scholars.

13.3.1851

signed J. S. Towse,
Minister.

The surviving parts of the south and east walls of the first Nonconformist chapel, built 1795.

[Martyn Kirby]

OTHER RELIGIOUS GROUPS

Methodists were being mentioned in records by 1764, and John Wesley made many visits to the East Riding between 1752 and 1790. Wesleyan Methodism became a very strong religious movement in this area, although Primitive Methodism, which arrived in 1819, became a stronger force: by the middle of the century the East Riding had become proportionally the strongest area in the county for Primitive Methodism. In Thorngumbald houses were registered for worship in 1796, 1811 and again in 1831, obviously for non-conformist worship.

The first chapel to be built in the village was erected in 1795 by Sir Samuel Standidge who also built a minister's house and schoolroom and gave an endowment of six acres of land called Clot Close to support it. These were given by Standidge's heirs to Fish Street Congregational Chapel, Hull, after his death in 1801, by a conveyance dated 1809. Thorngumbald chapel was taken over by the Primitive Methodists by 1890 and was closed as a chapel in 1936.

During the Second World War it was evidently used as the headquarters of the local Home Guard, and after the war the local football team used it as a recreation hall for some years before its partial demolition in the 1960s. The remains of this chapel, namely parts of the south and east walls, still stand and are situated at the east side of Central Nurseries, opposite the Hall. There was also a cottage just to the east of the chapel, on the Main Road, known as Standidge Cottage, and most probably the former minister's house or the schoolroom mentioned earlier; this was destroyed about the same time.

An Independent minister is recorded in the village in 1795, when it is said, 'The Reverend J. Morley lived and ministered there'. He was the first minister of the new chapel. In 1801 Mr. Morley moved to Hope Street, Hull, and was succeeded by Rev. William Stephenson who stayed until 1815, to be succeeded in turn by Rev. R. Kirkus until 1832. By 1846 Rev. William Bettison, a Cornishman, was minister, and he is mentioned again in 1851 and 1887 — a long ministry: he would have presumably retired or died soon after, being 77 years old by this date, and there is no further mention of a resident minister at Thorngumbald.

There is some evidence that the Methodists took over the chapel before this time, although it was not sold to them until 1890. It is most likely they were henceforth served by a circuit minister.

The Wesleyans built a chapel in 1840 on the present site. It was rebuilt in 1904 and is still in use today. It appears to have been altered very little since this date, although there was an interesting occurrence in January, 1985, when, during repairs to the front wall, a 'time capsule' was discovered behind a stone in the wall, containing details of the stone-laying ceremony in 1904. Contents also included a penny coin minted in 1903, two newspapers and a list of chapel officials and participants at the time. These were replaced along with the following from the present time: a *Hull Daily Mail*, a *Holderness Gazette*, a Parish *Newsletter*, a list of present chapel members, and some modern coins.

In 1967 a Jennings electric organ replaced the original Forster and Andrews organ which was sent to Burstwick Methodist Chapel for storage. However, it had to be scrapped, as mice had got into it — some form of religious rodent no doubt!

Incidentally the Jennings cannot have had the enduring qualities of its predecessor, as it also had to be replaced in 1973 by a Hammond organ.

Below are the religious census returns for 1851 for both chapels:

WESLEYAN METHODIST CHAPEL

When erected — 1840
Space available for worship — free sitting 40 — other sitting 40
Estimated number at Divine Service — evening 31/3/1851 — 39
Average attendance — 40
                    (signed) Thomas Smith of Thorngumbald — Steward.

INDEPENDENT CHAPEL

When erected — before 1800
Space available — free sitting 100 — other sitting 30
Attendance at 31/3/1851 — morning 25
                                evening 30
                                Sunday Scholars 21
Average attendance —   morning 30
                                evening 40
                                Sunday Scholars 20
                    (signed) W. Bettison — Minister.

Below is an interesting item from the *Hull Advertiser* of 24 April, 1840:

THORNGUMBALD

On Monday last a Sunday School Feast in connection with the Independent Chapel was held in the house of Mr. J. F. Butter in the above village. Thirty five children were regaled with tea, as well as all the male and female teachers. After tea the children were catechised and suitably addressed by several gentlemen who attended for that purpose, and afterwards received thanks, which consisted of Bibles, Testaments, and other books according to their respective merits. This school is now in a highly prosperous condition attributable to the steady attention of the teachers and to the kind patronage of Mrs. Butter who at her own expense regularly provides two Feasts for the school each year.

Thorngumbald 1750-1850.

1 WEST HOAD
2 SUMMERGANGS LEYS
3 FAR FIVE STANGS
4 WHEATHOLM LEYS
5 WHEATHOLM
6 PLAIN ASKHOLM
7 LONG CLOSE
8 BRATT FURZE
9 WEST FLATT
10 MEAN PIECE
11 MEAN GORDALES
12 EAST HOAD

DRAINAGE

There is no doubt that drainage in this area was, and still is, of the utmost importance; the whole area around Thorngumbald is only slightly above sea level and, as mentioned before, in earlier times a larger portion of land would be under water, particularly in the southernmost parts of the village which were all marshlands. These wet pastures could probably only be fully grazed in the summer months.

There are numerous references to the wet and poor land of Holderness, and indeed the first Lord of Holderness, Odo, complained to William the Conqueror that, 'Holderness was exceedingly barren and unfruitful and brought nothing but wild oats'. This was heeded by William who awarded him further lands at Lindsey in Lincolnshire. The other well-known reference to Holderness comes from Chaucer's *Summoner's Tale,* in the lines, 'Lordyngs, there is in Yorkshire as I gesse, a messhy contree calld Holdernesse'.

This area of low-lying marshy land set obvious drainage problems, not least of which was the fact that Holderness is bordered on three sides with high ground, leaving the natural drainage of the area into the Humber. This fact was compounded around the 10th century, when the salt flats in the Humber began to silt up. This was encouraged by embankment in the following centuries, and in turn led to much flooding.

The first mention that we find of drainage in our area is the Scurthdyke — the dyke that drained the northern part of our village and had its source at Humbleton Beck, extending through to Burstwick, where at a place called Parraknoke (possibly meaning sharp bend — at Burstwick South Park) it divided into two streams, one of which, Parkdyke, ran by Ryehill, Thorngumbald and Stockholm to Hedon Fleet.

This leg of the drain was the larger of the two and was twenty-feet wide and ten-feet deep and was probably cut by the Lords of Holderness who had moved to Burstwick from their original castle at Skipsea in the early 14th century; most people agree that this dyke or drain was probably navigable and was very likely used to convey timber and goods from their new home in Burstwick to the recently created port of Hedon.

Not only must this dyke have made a considerable difference to the drainage in the northern Carrs of Thorngumbald, but it would also remove some of the waters that passed through the south marshes by the dyke we now call Thorngumbald Drain. This also runs along the northern part of Thorngumbald from east to west before turning south and crossing the Main Road just west of the cemetery, from where it originally ran to a sluice at Thorneycrofts and hence into the Humber; this outlet was obstructed by the growth of Cherry Cob Sands in the 18th century and the sluice had to be moved in the 1750s.

In 1764 the area drained by Thorneycrofts Drain was removed from the jurisdiction of the Court of Sewers for the east part of the East Riding and was given to a newly created Thorngumbald Drainage Authority which cut a new drain in 1766 well to the west of the sand banks at its present outfall in Paull. Thorngumbald Drainage Authority is still in being and the old drain is also still in existence, meandering its way from Thorneycrofts through the south of the old marshlands to the junction of the new leg just south of Villa Farm, Thorngumbald.

The first mention of these drains I can find is in the records of the Court of Sewers for the east part of the East Riding in 1365, which state:

> And from the aforesaid field of Ryhill, near the field of Thorngumband, and thence even to Stockholme Land, and so even to the aforesaid close near Headon Fleit, and is unsufficient, which ought to be twenty feet broad and ten foot deep, and ought to be repaired by Ryhill, Camerington Thorngumband and others which have their soil abutting, even to the aforesaid Headon Fleit on the south side, and the Lord of Burstwick on the north side.

The Court of Sewers makes another mention of Thorngumbald in 1367 and refers to a sewer [drain], 'Bernardsleit'. [See Communications — Roads.]

The other factor affecting drainage at Thorngumbald was that the village borders the Humber at its southern extremity or rather it did before the creation of the growths and sandbanks on the river banks, now known as Cherry Cob Sands. The drying out of these areas of the Saltmarsh was encouraged during the 10th, 11th and 12th centuries by the embankment of the river; Meaux Abbey had a number of granges in the area and the Lords of Holderness owned Little Humber. South of Old Little Humber is probably the line of the original bank that kept the river at bay.

We know from documents of the Court of Sewers that in 1660 these banks were between four and six-feet high, existed along the whole of the Humber shoreline, and were protected on the Humber side by breakwaters. It is evident that this embankment was moved southwards over the centuries as more and more of the saltmarshes began to silt up, particularly from the middle of the 17th century when the North Channel around Sunk Island began to silt up. In 1744 20,000 acres were reclaimed at Sunk Island, although it was still an island and reached via a bridge.

One of the problems this silting produced was that drains which had emptied into the North Channel were no longer efficient: the reason Thorneycrofts Drain was eventually moved away from the North Channel in 1766, as mentioned earlier. Keyingham Drain, which took the waters from Ryehill Drain and the lands to the east of the village, was also experiencing the same problems, as its outfall was also into the North Channel. In the 18th century this led to great flooding in the area, and in 1730 a new clough was built to alleviate this problem. In 1772 an act was obtained to remove Keyingham Drain from the Court of Sewers to a new body, the Keyingham Drainage Authority, which moved the clow to a site known as No Man's Friend, near to the eastern part of the newly-reclaimed Cherry Cob Sands.

This seems to have worked for a number of years, but by 1796-7 a Mr. Chapman was commissioned to report on the silting, and recommended moving No Man's Friend Clow and deepening and cleansing the channel. The cost was over £16,000 and the recommendation appears not to have been adopted. In 1802 an act was obtained to extend the drain from No Man's Friend Clow into the River Humber at Stone Creek, as by this time the North Channel was rapidly silting up and, as the map shows, Sunk Island was attached to the mainland by 1850.

One event of recent interest has been the embanking of the Humber from Paull to Spurn Point, which shows that the holding back of the waters of the Humber is just as important today as it was all those centuries ago.

A faded but evocative view showing Gray's shop on the south side of Main Road, opposite the modern Crescent.

Two unusually quiet scenes at Thorngumbald Show, 1905.

COMMUNICATIONS — ROADS

The first mention of roads in Thorngumbald is in the will of John Garton, a Hull merchant who, as mentioned earlier, had left £5 to St. Mary's Church in 1455; at the same time he left £5 for 'the road inter Thorn and Hedon'.

The roads in every village up to this period had belonged to, and been the responsibility of, the Lords of the Manor, who would merely instruct their tenants to provide the labour to make any repairs required.

By the Tudor period the manorial system started to decline, and by 1555 the 'Act for the Amending of Highways' was passed, putting the onus on the parish: four days' gratuitous labour per annum was called for from parishioners, and two 'honest persons' were to be elected each year to serve as surveyors to superintend and organise the work. This appears to have applied to the cottagers only, the better-off contributing the carts and equipment needed and possibly some extra labour. The law was altered in 1563 when the compulsory labour was increased to six days of eight hours' duration; the quality of labour, as in most cases when it is unpaid, must have been doubtful, for in the mid-1500s William Harrison in his *Description of England* remarked: 'The rich do so cancel their portion and the poor so loiter in their labours that, of all the six, scarcely two good days are performed.'

The roads were still little more than dirt tracks, and, when one considers the marshy lands around Thorngumbald, must have been in a very bad state indeed by modern standards. The Vicar of Holy Trinity, Hull, reported in 1707 that the roads in Holderness were next to impassable in winter and that some people who had ventured through them had lost their lives.

Roads were improved considerably during the 1700s by two major steps: the improvement of drainage and the turnpike trusts. The first turnpike road to benefit Thorngumbald was the Hull-Preston-Hedon road of 1745 which had toll bars at Summergangs, Wyton and Sacred Gate. It was extended by the Hedon-Patrington Haven Turnpike Trust formed in 1761. These trusts had power to collect tolls at the bars for the upkeep of the roads; the parish still had to contribute towards the roads' upkeep but this was much less than previously, and the advantage of this system was that the people who used the roads the most paid the most.

Unfortunately, by the late 1800s, most of these trusts were in debt, and the Hedon-Patrington Haven road was dis-turnpiked in 1874 and passed to the County Council completely in 1888. One of the major factors in the decline of the turnpike trusts was the emergence of the railways. The building of the Hull-Withernsea railway in 1854 must have speeded the decline of the Hedon-Patrington Trust, although Thorngumbald did not enjoy a station on the line. The nearest was situated at Ryehill, half way between Thorngumbald and Burstwick.

In 1367 at a search taken at Skipsea into the state of sewers (drains) it was said: 'A certain sewer called Bernardsleit lieth between Thorngumband and Thornincroft, and the Manor of Little Humber, lies in the walls of Humber with one gate, and is defective; neither is the gate cleansed, and ought to be repaired in the middle part by the Lord of Little Humber, and the other parts by the Lord of Thorngumband and the Abbot of Thornton, and now is void, from which defect there is a certain highway called Hollgate, and another, which is called Thormana, and they are stopped, and the part and pasture thereunto adjoining are drown'd.'

One assumes from this that Hollgate is the Hull-Withernsea road, and Thormana the Thorn-Paull road. Some of the older village inhabitants can still remember this road being 'gated', these gates having to be opened to pass through. The road from Thorngumbald to Stone Creek did not exist in 1772 when Jefferys made his map of East Yorkshire, although a short section existed from the cross roads possibly as far as the left hand bend on the corner of which used to be Bellcroft Well; it was extended in 1757 during the enclosure of lands and was then called New Lane. This road, which is now called Bellcroft Lane, certainly looks a recently created road, as it is perfectly straight for most of its length.

One other small road is mentioned at the time of the 1757 enclosure, Hurd Lane, which led to a pasture called West Hoad and thence to Greenmarsh. Many people in the village can remember a public right of way from the Main Road on the opposite side to the present cemetery but slightly to the east. It was large enough to give access for large steam engines, and ended at Garth Ends Drain. A public footpath then continued to Paull Road. It would seem in all probability that this was the route which had been Hurd Lane, as it would have run into the north-eastern corner of West Hoad pasture.

A mounting-block mile stone, probably dating from the turnpike road of 1761, now in the grounds of Thorngumbald Hall.

[Martyn Kirby]

26

SAMUEL STANDIDGE AND THE HALL

If Thorngumbald had to name its most famous resident, it would have to be Samuel Standidge. He was born in Bridlington in 1725, served an apprenticeship at sea, and by 1749 was Captain Samuel Standidge, a merchant as well as a seaman. Standidge is recognised as the father of the Hull whaling industry in the Georgian period when he equipped a ship at his own expense in 1767 and sent it out to the whaling grounds off Greenland. It was said at the time by other merchants that this was an act 'bordering on insanity'. However, the voyage was a great success, and with the new processes of refining the oil, and through his business acumen he became a rich man. Standidge at this time lived in High Street, Hull, along with the Maisters, Blaydes and other wealthy families. His property ran down to the river and is given as 186 yards long by 65 yards wide. The site was 1, High Street, now derelict.

The late 1700s see many of the rich families of Hull starting to build country residences. When one considers that the whaling insdustry was now in full swing in the port, the smell from the oil processing industry must have been nauseating, and one can understand the motivation behind this movement. Standidge decided to build his country residence at Thorngumbald and in 1768 purchased 200 acres of land from John Hobman. By 1770 his mansion was built. It is said in various books that 20,000 bricks were taken from Newton Hospital for this purpose. (Newton Hospital had been one of the two leper colonies at Hedon and had been founded by William Le Gros. It was adjacent to the present Newton Garth Farm on the Hedon to Paull road, and was destroyed during the Reformation.)

It may not, however, be correct. Just before Standidge built the Hall, the records of the Hedon Haven Commissioners included an account for the purchase of 20,000 bricks to build a lockpit: it was never built and the idea was abandoned. As Standidge was one of the Commissioners it seems more probable that he acquired these bricks for his new mansion, rather than using secondhand bricks from a building destroyed 200 years earlier.

Standidge also bought other land and property in Thorngumbald and district. New York Farm, Preston, is said to have been purchased with the proceeds of one successful voyage to that city; Nova Scotia Farm also belonged to him, as did Stockholm, Greenmarsh, Southern Farm, Field Close, and Far Marsh in Thorngumbald. He also owned farms in Hedon and Burstwick and several of the garths opposite his Hall — Old Holm Garth, Green Marsh Close, Oxcraft Garth, Scotts Garth and West Garth.

Standidge was Sheriff of Hull in 1775, an alderman in 1794 and Mayor in 1795. He was also Warden of Trinity House in the same year, a position he also held in 1777, 1782, 1795 and 1800. During his year as Mayor, Captain

Thorngumbald Hall, 1990. *[Martyn Kirby]*

A folly now in the front garden of Thorngumbald Hall — constructed from stone removed from Paull Fort. *[Martyn Kirby]*

Standidge, as he was then, entertained Prince William of Gloucester [later William IV] when His Royal Highness visited the town on 4 November; the following year he was knighted by George III! He also became involved in the dispute between prominent local landowners over the ownership of the reclaimed land at Sunk Island. He attested for the Crown lessee that he had sailed around the island by Stone Creek (the North Channel) when chased by a privateer — surely further help towards his knighthood! The Crown won the case. He was granted Russian nobility in c.1790 for supplying the Empress Catherine with 53 transport ships for use in her war against Turkey and also received an Imperial Decoration (a Maltese Cross in gold set with topaz). Standidge died in 1801 and left £75,000 in his will, an enormous sum in those days. There is a tablet inscribed to his memory on the west wall of St. Mary's Church, Lowgate, Hull, and he is buried in the north aisle of the church.

Standidge had no son and at the death of Lady Standidge the Hall at Thorngumbald passed to their only daughter, Mary, the wife of William Thornton and then to her grandson, Samuel Standidge Slater, who sold it and approximately six acres to Edward Sheldon, who in turn sold it to Abraham Dunn in 1827. Thorngumbald Hall, as it was then called, was bought by John Farrer Butter in 1828. The same John Butter bought 96 acres from the Holme family estate in 1854. Butter died in 1866, J. H. Denniss bought it along with 223 acres in 1867, then sold it again to William Marsden and R. S. Dixon in 1879. In 1880-1 the house was demolished and rebuilt in its present neo-Jacobean style by Charles Hargitt Johnson who had purchased it the previous year. C. H. Johnson died in 1924 and his son, C. R. Johnson, sold it in 1938 to C. Markham and Sons who divided it the following year. It was purchased in March, 1944, by Albert McDonald Willey whose occupation was given as a taxi proprietor. Willey sold the Hall in May, 1946, to Cecil Rhodes, a wholesale fruit merchant of Withernsea, who in turn sold it in May, 1957, to David Cooke, a company director. The Hall stayed in the Cooke family until 1981 when the west wing was sold to Mr. M. A. McArdle, the present owner, who has since converted it into a residential home for the elderly. The east wing was sold to Mr. I. Lanham, the present occupier, in 1986. Incidentally, although a road in the village is named after Standidge, an incorrect spelling, *Standage*, is used.

An extract from the *Hull News* of Saturday, 8 April, 1905, is printed below:

> Thorngumbald Hall is of recent construction. The building, which is situated on the old turnpike road from Hull to Patrington, was erected by the present owner and occupier, Major C. Johnson, about twenty-five years ago. It is a fine up-to-date mansion and fitted up with modern requirements. The gardens are very pretty, and in one portion at the back of the Hall is a model 'Stonehenge' which was made out of some boulders of stone that came from Paull Fort after

some alterations. A wall, described as the finest in Holderness, separates the Hall grounds from the highway. Major Johnson has been away for some time, but it is anticipated that his return to the Hall will take place this spring.'

The fine entrance to Thorngumbald Hall, with the monogram, 'CHJ' commemorating Charles Hargitt Johnson who rebuilt the Hall, 1880-1.

[*Martyn Kirby*]

EDUCATION

In 1743 it was said that 'in Thorngumbald there is no charity school within the Chapelry, but there is a school taught by one John Holmes who teaches about twenty-five children to read English and write, and instructs them in Church catechism.' We can imagine that this teaching would be very rudimentary and would be no more than a few hours a week. As there was no school building at this time, it would have to be carried out in some private house or premises. This was to change, however, in 1795 when Sir Samuel Standidge built a school alongside his new Congregational chapel, presumably the school which in 1833 was classed as a mixed school and had six pupils, supported by the parents. Mary Harrison was teaching at this school in 1851.

J. F. Butter of Thorngumbald Hall built a new school in 1860 on the site of what is now the Church Institute and it was conveyed by Butter to his two nieces, Jane and Elizabeth Dooby, who resided in Thorngumbald. An Independent school is mentioned in 1870, the one attended by 20 boys and girls on inspection day in 1871. Four years later, Thorngumbald United School District was formed, including the parishes of Ryehill and Camerton, and a new Board School was built in Ryehill parish — now the present village hall. It had been taken over by East Riding County Council in 1903.

Two of the school record books have survived from the last century and a few interesting items from them are listed below:

1880	Receipts	
	Payments from overseers of the poor	£142. 15s. 2d.
	Grants from Educational Council	32. 10s.
	School Fees	35. 0 4d.
	Other grants	5s.
		[Other amounts not quoted]
	Total	£262. 9s. 5d.

Payments included
William Aspen — school master,
one month's salary   £8. 6s. 8d.
                          [Other amounts not quoted]
                    Year's Total   £108. 6s. 8d.

At a meeting of the Thorngumbald United District School Board held on the 8th day of April 1891 in the Board Room, Ryehill.

Two school groups, undated but both early 20th century; the upper one showing 'Cocky' Wright is probably the older.

[Reproduced by kind permission of Mr. E. Franks, Peck's Nurseries]

Present: Mr. M. H. Goundrill — Chairman
Mr. K. I. Hosdell
Mr. I. Leonard
Mr. N. Walgate

The Clerk reported. Proposed by Mr. Hosdell and seconded by Mr. Walgate that summonses be taken out against Jas. Gardner for the non attendance of his children Herbert and Harriet, Robert Lawton for the non attendance of his children William and Robert, and Acey for the non attendance of his child William. Carried.

M. H. Goundrill, Chairman

8th day of July 1891

The Clerk reported that the summonses issued against Gardner and Lawton were heard at Patrington on the 13th June last, and in Gardner's case a fine of 1s. in each case was made. And in Lawton's cases an attendance order made.

In 1888 Aspen had left and John Wright had been appointed as headmaster at a salary of £66 13s 0d per year, a considerable reduction. However, by 1899 Wright's salary had risen to £105 9s 0d, almost back to the sum of 20 years before. Wright continued as headmaster for many years, and there are people who can still remember 'Cocky Wright', as he was known. Wright was a very stern disciplinarian and most people remember this side of him, rather than his teaching skills. He came to an untimely end, however, for he was found drowned in a large rainwater tub at the rear of the Camerton cottage to which he had retired. Wright was headmaster until 1 April, 1924, a long stay of well over 30 years.

During this time he saw many changes to the school. In 1903 a cloakroom was added; in 1909, 520 square yards of land were purchased at the cost of one shilling per square yard as an extension; and the same year a soft water system (rain water) was installed at a cost of £485 0s 0d (it included a cast-iron tank that appears to have been installed underground: I wonder if it is still there somewhere!). During these improvements lessons were moved temporarily to the Village Institute. 1911 saw the introduction of domestic lessons for girls. Mrs Wright took these lessons — she is mentioned some years later requesting a salary increase.

Mr J. H. Woodfield replaced Wright, staying for just over a year before taking up the position of County Librarian. He in turn was succeeded by Mr George Gramley on 1 February, 1926.

Electric lighting was installed during his headmastership in 1930 at a cost of £9 5s. 6d.

Mr Bramley was replaced by Mr Alan Hardwick on 1 September, 1930. He did not stay long, however, his time as headmaster being beset with problems, and he was replaced temporarily by John Wright who returned from retirement for a few months until John Sydney Andrews was appointed on 1 September, 1931. 'Gaffer Andrews', as he was known to the children, was to see the school water supply connected to the Hull Corporation water main in 1933, and a bathroom and hot water installed at the school house the same year. A cycle shelter was provided in 1934, as many children had to cycle 2-3 miles to school, and the cycles were obstructing the entrance and corridors. Andrews was also Chairman of the Parish Council, and it was he who signed the deeds when the cemetery was bought in 1937. He resigned when he was appointed headmaster to Hessle Church of England School.

Mr Sydney Ballance replaced him on 1 September, 1940. 'Billy Ballance' stayed until 21 December, 1962, when he retired. His wife was also a teacher at the school for much of this time, and he was to witness a unique situation during January, 1956. The school logbook records the following words: 'We have an occasion of rarity in the annals of this school as well as the East Riding, where the staff consists of Mr Ballance, Mrs Ballance (Sen.), Mrs Ballance (Jun.), Miss Ballance (cook).' This had been brought about by two factors: the new South Holderness School had opened at Preston in January, 1955, and all the senior pupils had been transferred, leaving fewer teachers, and Billy Ballance's son (who was also a teacher) had married Miss P. T. Dalby who was then the infant teacher at the school.

Mr Ballance retired on 21 December, 1962, to be succeeded by Mr A. S. Daniels, at the commencement of the January term, 1963. He was to see the most dramatic change to education in the village this century when the new Grange Road School was opened on 7 September, 1964. Mr Daniels stayed 9½ years, being replaced by Mr. P. Scott, 1973-1976, Mr R. Helliwell, 1977-1981, and the present head, Mr E. C. Murray, from that date.

Although the new school was supposed to replace the old Board School, the influx of young people into the village with families made the new school overcrowded almost as soon as it was built, and the old school was used intermittently for many years as an overflow until well into the 1970s when new classrooms were added to the Grange Road School. Even these were to prove inadequate, and a new Infant School was built at the bottom of Plumtree Road in January, 1979, Mrs Eastwood becoming the first headmistress. She retired at Easter, 1988, to be succeeded by the present headmistress, Mrs C. M. Crawford.

Mrs Eastwood also had the unique record of having served in all the three village schools during her teaching career.

The old Board School appears to have had three classes during most of its time, the headmaster taking the seniors, with the junior and infant classes being taken by women teachers, Emily S. Duffill was already teaching by 1903 and was to stay as the infant teacher until 1936 when she died suddenly in the garden of her house opposite the school.

Francis Pickering was a supplementary teacher in 1903 and was replaced in 1905 by Mary Fewster. In 1906 it was recommended that her salary be increased from £35 0s. 0d. to £50 0s. 0d. after she had passed the King's Scholarship Examination.

Harriet Walker followed Mary Fewster in 1920, and Dorothy M. Wright who, people tell me, came from Cottingham, replaced Emily Duffill. She was to follow John Andrews and go to Hessle Church of England School in 1940. Miss K. Stephenson started in 1938 and left in 1942 to take up an appointment at Withernsea Central School, Mrs Snowden, the infant teacher in 1941, left in 1947 to go to Patrington School, and Mrs Walker started the same year as junior teacher, leaving in 1949, Mr Ellis succeeding her. Other teachers to follow at the school were Miss Dalby, Mrs Ferris, Mrs Riley, Miss Acey, Miss Thompson, Miss Hodgson, Mrs Butters, Mrs Greenlees, and Mrs Eastwood, the last three moving to the new school when it opened in 1964. Mrs Ballance, as mentioned earlier, also taught at the school during most of her husband's headmastership, starting as an uncertificated teacher about 1943, later becoming qualified, and finally retiring in 1957.

The Board School had places for 120 pupils, but this figure was never reached until the last years, the numbers being 80-90 pupils.

Another interesting feature the records show is the number of times the school was closed because of epidemics, whooping cough, measles, diphtheria and influenza, all closing the school at different times, particularly in the earlier part of the century, sometimes even twice a year. Parents take note and remember your innoculations!

The Victorian Board School, now the Village Hall.   [Martyn Kirby]

Crooked Cottage (right): the single-storey building was originally a smithy, later a joiner's shop.

The Wesleyan Chapel, 1904, on the site of a chapel built in 1840 (left) and (right) the Church Institute 1908, on the site of a school built 1860. [Martyn Kirby]

AGRICULTURE

The early agriculture of Thorngumbald was dependent on a number of key factors: the height of the land above sea level, the efficiency of the banks of the Humber, and the standards of drainage employed. Although later improvements have made it one of the country's richest areas of agricultural land, this was not always the case and in earlier times the village lands were constantly flooded, as many reports confirm. The very names of areas of the village themselves testify to this: Far Marsh, Greenmarsh, Summergangs (Summer Water Pasture) and North Carrs all indicate that these lands were probably under water, and only in the summertime would be good grazing lands.

The first traceable land transactions after the Domesday Book evidence concern the two carucates of land owned by the Gumbaud family — in the 1280s, and between 1197-1210 when Adam of Thorn granted 70 acres at Stockholm to Meaux Abbey. We also know that about this time Aumale Abbey held meadow and pasture land in Thorngumbald.

The marshes to the south side of the village provided the common pastures, and presumably it was on these that Aumale Abbey grazed a flock of 80 sheep in the 12th century. In the 15th century sheep were pastured in Greenmarsh, and cattle in Far Marsh, while Thorneycrofts was divided into closes of meadows and pastures. Other pastures were West Hoad, East Hoad, and Hurd Pasture which comprised four separate areas: Summergangs, Furdales, Askham Hill and East Carrs. The meadows were the North Carrs, Riggs, Plain Askham, Bratt Furze, Mean Gordales, Five Far Stengs, Summergangs Leys, Wheat Holm, Wheat Holm Leys, West Flats, Long Close and Mean Piece.

The arable land was mainly in the open fields of the village which stretched right along the north side of the main road and were bounded in the east by the present Ryehill drain and in the west ending at about the present cemetery. The northern boundary was just beyond the present North Carrs drain: in all a total of about 380 acres.

The old system of farming was inefficient. Farmers and cottagers had small strips of land in both the meadows and arable fields. Considerable co-operation was necessary to ensure the smooth running of the open field system and enclosure was a way of grouping these strips together into more compact holdings.

In 1757 the remaining common lands in Thorngumbald were enclosed by agreement and award (some had already been enclosed earlier). This act would today be classed as a rationalisation of the village lands. What happened in general was: the larger landowners of the village called a meeting and drew up a petition asking Parliament for the right to introduce a bill. Usually, provided four or five landowners were in favour, the act was passed and Commissioners and Surveyors were appointed to begin their task of rationalising the land.

The Commissioners' decisions were legally binding, and, as they were usually appointed by the large landowners, these appear to have gained even more land. It seems to have been another case of the rich getting richer and the poor getting poorer. There are many instances where the Commissioners were criticised for their failure to look after the small landowner; this bias is understandable when you consider that sometimes they were in the employ of one of the landowners concerned. It must be said, however, that the enclosures at Thorngumbald appear to have been carried out reasonably fairly.

The Commissioners of Thorngumbald were: Joseph Thompson of Hull, Robert Bell of Hedon, and John Dickinson of Warter.

The Surveyors were: Charles Tate and Peter Neville.

The amount of land assessed was 1,001 acres and the awards were made on 12 December, 1757.

A list of landowners and their allotments [allocations] of land by the Commissioners follows:

NAME	ALLOTMENT/ ACREAGE	OCCUPATION	ABODE
John Holmes	26	Yeoman	Thorngumbald
John Hobman	135	Merchant & Gentleman	Danzig
Mary Fawsitt	160	Widow	
Waite Walker	65	Gentleman	Hedon
John Carvill	27	Gentleman	Bower House Hill Paull
Bacon Moritt	60	Cay Wood	Yorks
Roger Gee	339	Gentleman	Keyingham Marsh
Marmaduke Brown	12	Gentleman	Burstwick
Charles Pool	8	Gentleman	Burstwick
Thomas Hutchinson	17½	Gentleman	Ryehill
John Tivilton	1	Yeoman	Thorn
William Thornton	1	Merchant	Hull

One note of interest is John Hobman's description as a 'Merchant of Danzig', although the Hobmans were a well-known Hull family of this time. It was common practice for these merchant families to send a member overseas to one of their principal trading ports. It should be noted that these measurements are not an exact copy of the original awards. In the original document they are noted in poles and perches along with acres; to simplify this I have approximated them. Anyone with a thirst for this kind of knowledge can find them in the Humberside County Record Office at Beverley.

Until the late 1600s the main crops were oats and wheat, although some rape and flax were being grown in the village. In the 1800s the main crops were mustard, wheat, beans, oats, clover and turnips. In the mid-16th century the wool tythes were let to Kirkstall Abbey and later the Crown; these then passed to Sir Christopher Hatton, who sold them in 1586 to Sir Henry Constable. Thereafter they passed down the Constable family. Other tythes were held by the Mandor family during the 17th and 18th centuries. The commutation of tythes on these lands in 1849 brought the Mandor family 16 shillings for 13 acres; £15 to the Constable family; and Richard Boyle was awarded a rent charge of £89 for corn, hay and lamb tythes.

There were also several fields in Thorngumbald that had originally been confiscated by Henry VIII during his arguments with the church. In 1704 Queen Anne set up a fund to use the revenue from these lands throughout England. It became known as Queen Anne's Bounty and was used mainly to supplement the income of the poorer clergy. In 1948 Queen Anne's Bounty was incorporated into the Church Commission for England, which still administers these fields.

Sir John Lister, in his will dated 20 December, 1640, left land at Thorngumbald and 'Bore House Hill', Paull, to support his 'Hospital in Hull': this was to provide income for pensions for the poor, and wages for the clerk to the Trustees, and a preacher. He also instructed that a habitation was to be built for six poor men and women. He endowed a building with six low rooms to be built in Trinity churchyard, also another building with four rooms for a preacher of the church, together with a pump and handsome brick wall surrounding the paved courtyard. This almshouse was rebuilt on its original site on the south side of South Churchside in 1779 and was conveyed in 1869 to Mr. Edwin Davis, who rebuilt the almshouse in Park Street at this time. It appears that the vacated site was used for the Edwin Davis store destroyed by a Zeppelin raid during World War I.

In 1822, at the enclosure of Paull, 31 acres were awarded in Thorngumbald to the Lister Trustees in exchange for property at Boreas Hill. Of those 31 acres, 20 were sold in 1970, the remainder, now the village allotments, were owned by Hull United Charities, the Lister Vestees, up to 1989, when the allotments were purchased by the Parish Council. These allotments have been in existence since at least the 1890s, when allotment land is mentioned on the north side of the Main Road. It appears the land was extended during the First World War to assist the war effort. Other allotment land existed in the 1880s and early 1900s and was situated on Paull Road near to the entrance to Greenmarsh Road.

THE VILLAGE PEOPLE

To trace the inhabitants of the village up to the last century is not easy. We know that the Gumbaud family were the first Lords of the Manor, and they probably resided in the village, although there is no proof they actually did. The Lay Subsidies of Edward I (1297) give the tax payers as Simon Fabro, Waltero Schippe, Simon Bridde and Petro Longo. This at least gives us the names of the villagers who were wealthy enough to pay this tax.

Fortunately, in the Borthwick Institute, York, *The Easter Book of Paull alias Paghill Tythes* contains a section for 1604 which lists Thorngumbald separately, and gives the following as paying tythes:

Robert Buckles, Roger Ramshaw, William Holmes, William Tiplady, Thomas Brown, John Jackson, William Brown, John Keeley, Mary Marshall, William Carvill, H. Carvill, John Tivilton, Marmaduke Curtis, Richard Parson, John Halland, Widow North, Francis Ombler, Mr. Jackson, William Jackson, Mary Lockington, John Stansfield, William Killick, Francis Hill, George Roe and Mr. Levitt.

This would appear to be an almost complete list of the families who inhabited the village at this time, and gives us the first glimpse of the 'ordinary' people of the village.

The Holme family mentioned above were to feature prominently in the records of Thorngumbald. They were a part of the family of that name who lived at Paull Holme and were involved in Thorngumbald affairs from at least 1385, when an inquiry at Hedon commanded William Holme to 'remove to Paghill (Paull) and meddle no further' with certain land and rents in Thorngumbald.

The church terriers (records) of the 1600s give some of the names of the churchwardens and officials of this time. A William Holme is mentioned in these several times, along with Marmaduke Brown, John Marshall, John Kitchen, James Brown, William Chadwell, Roger Ramshaw and William Tiplady.

As you can see, there are family names which are starting to be repeated and it is now possible to see the village people begin to 'come to life' as individuals, rather than a collection of facts and figures.

The land tax assessments of the late 1700s and early 1800s give us the proprietors and occupiers of land in the village. The earliest I can find is for 1750 but it only lists proprietors. The assessment of 1793 is the first to include both, and is given below:

The 1800s are a much more productive time for information. In 1823 Baines published their *Directory*, which included a small section on Thorngumbald. This was to be followed in 1840 by White's, in 1843 by Pigot & Co, and in 1851 by Slater's. As they shed more light on the village at this time the latter two are printed below:

PIGOT & CO. 1843   266 people

Todd Sarah	Postmistress	Garton John	Retailer of beer
Ellis Thom.	Blacksmith	Roper William	Black Horse - Pub.
Smith Thom.	Blacksmith	Chambers Thomas	Tailor
Willingham Geo.	Blacksmith	Garton Anne	Grocer
		Garton John	Wheelwright
Elletson James	Shoemaker		
Hastings Richard	Shoemaker		
Mitcheson John	Bricklayer	Highland William	Wheelwright
Call James	Gardener seedsman	Burnham William	Farrier
Peck Samuel	Gardener seedsman		

COACHES
Coaches from Hull every Tuesday, Thursday, Friday at 6.15pm, Sat. at 9.15am.
Coaches from Patrington same as above.

LETTERS
Letters by Horse post, 5.30pm. Dispatch, 7.45am. Receive.

SLATER'S 1851

GENTRY
Bettison Rev.
Butter, J. F.
Smith Mrs. Jane

Harrison Mary	School Teacher	Call James	Seedsman/Gardener
Smith Thomas	Blacksmith	Elletson James & John	Seedsman/Gardener
Willingham Geo.	Blacksmith	Peck George & Simon	Seedsman/Gardener
Found John	Shoemaker	Newton Thomas	Royal Mail
Rawson Thomas	Shoemaker	Hastings Edward	Grocer/General
Pickering Richard	Bricklayer	Newton Thomas	Grocer/General
Appelby John	Seedsman/Gardener	Robinson William	Taylor

Vice — Chapel of Ease   Rev. James Samuel Jones

Independent Chapel   Rev. William Bettison

CARRIERS William Spark and Thomas Smith. From Thorngumbald Tues. & Friday

COACHES from Hedon-Patrington
The Royal Mail every morning, from The Sun 9.30am, The Express every PM at 4.30 The Rocket at every PM 4.30, The Tiger, The Red Rover every Tuesday at 4.30pm.

POST OFFICE   Robert Island Postmaster
Letters arrive from Hull 9 am. Despatch at 5.10 pm.

Slater's (1851) also gives a figure for the village population and it is amazing how constant this remained until the 1960s. The first record of village population is the Poll Tax of 1377, returning 77 payers. The 1672 Hearth Tax returns list 26 households. This gives a better idea of population, but is still not informative above the size of the families. As mentioned previously, there were 21 families in Archbishop Herring's Returns of 1743. Poulson's *History of Holderness* lists the population as follows: 1801 — 190 people; 1811 — 215 people; 1821 — 259 people; 1831 - 266 people. The 1851 census return gives more detail i.e. 142 males and 136 females, a total of 278. The 1881 census lists 135 males and 132 females, a total of 267. The total for 1901 was 272 people and the same in 1931. Even in 1961 there was a similar total.

An intriguing example of tumbled gabling incorporated into the end wall of Crooked Cottage, Main Road.
[Martyn Kirby]

THE FARMS

The village relied heavily on its agricultural roots as did any country village of the time. In the mid-1800s, of the 53 families living in the village, 43 were engaged in agriculture, nine in trade and manufacturing, and one in another occupation. How different from the village of today, where, apart from the farmers and their families, we would be hard pressed to find more than a handful engaged directly in agriculture. The farmers were always the main employers of labour, with many of the village tradespeople supplying both their direct and ancillary needs.

We are fortunate in Thorngumbald that there is still in existence a tythe map for 1849 which shows the owners and occupiers of land and tenements in the village. This, coupled with the already mentioned census returns which listed everyone in the village at a given date, begins to give us a more complete picture of the village and the life of the people.

We must start by taking a look at the farms, the majority of which were spread along the Main Road, although a few were more distant, mostly in the old marshlands to the south of the village towards the Humber. Some of these farms no longer exist, and I thought it would be interesting to take a look at them first c.1840/50 and then move forward into this century.

One of the largest farms in the village in 1849 was undoubtedly Thorneycrofts, probably the furthest from the village centre, being situated at the southernmost extremity of the parish, on the left side of the road to Stone Creek (Far Marsh Road). In 1849 this farm comprised about 150 acres. It was owned by Richard G. Park and tenanted by Thomas Roydhouse, although a few years later it was occupied by the Leonard family, who then employed six people, including a Scottish governess.

The farm is very much the same today as it was then; in fact, the present farmhouse and adjoining stables are one of the very few listed buildings (grade II) in the village. The major change from that period is the use of the land. Most of it was formerly meadow and pasture. Today it is nearly all arable land.

Moving back towards the village along the same road, we find on the opposite side Nova Scotia Farm, sometimes known as Thorn Marsh Farm. Could this name be a relic of Sir Samuel Standidge, I wonder, for there was a tendency among the seafarers to name farms after places they had visited or had trading links with, and he did own a farm in the village called South Farm at one time? In 1849 this farm was occupied by Edward Goundrill and owned by a gentleman with the very un-English sounding name, George Schonswar (though he was a Hull merchant and M.P.).

A few hundred yards nearer the village was another farm owned by Sir Tatton Sykes and occupied by Thomas Jordan. The house has not been a farm in living memory and most people remember it as the farm foreman's house attached to Nova Scotia Farm; it has recently become a private residence.

As most of the other farms are, or were, almost adjacent to the Main Road, I thought it would be easier to look at them as if you were travelling from Hedon through the village on the old road.

The first farm we come to is on the left hand side of the road just beyond the Sacred Gate junction, standing well back from the road. This is Stockholm Farm and, as mentioned earlier, the lands belonging to this farm are recorded back to the 12th century. In 1849 it was owned and farmed by John Ingleby and comprised about 105 acres.

A little further on, and to the right of the Main Road, is a small lane which at the time of writing is being neatly bisected by the new Hedon Bypass. This lane leads to two farms; on the west fork lies Thorn Villa Farm, owned by Samuel Coverdale and occupied by Thomas Straker in 1849, but within a year or two the Fisher family had purchased this farm and also lived there. The descendants of this family still own and work this farm: a continuous span of nearly 140 years.

When I started this history and people became aware of my interest I was often asked questions on the village's past, one of the most common being, 'Is it true there was an abbey and castle in the village?' Well, residents, the news is not as expected. There was a castle in Thorngumbald and it was, indeed, very close to Thorn Villa Farm. A hedge-lined lane still leads to the original site, but it was not a grand mediaeval castle, just a small cottage that was inhabited by the farm foreman at Thorn Villa. It rejoiced in the name of Sparrow Castle; many people can remember it being demolished some time in the 1930s.

This site, however, could be quite old, as in the 1604 tythe book mentioned earlier, Thomas Hodgson is recorded as paying tythes for his garth, and Sparrow Garth. This cottage had one other claim to fame: in the early 1900s it was the weekend retreat of a Hull family named Nicholson. The son, Hubert, became a well-known author and in the autobiography of his early life, *Half My Days and Nights*, he mentions, with affection, his weekends spent at Sparrow Castle.

Incidentally, the abbey also existed, but, alas, was not the grand building usually associated with this name. I believe it to be another small cottage, now demolished, which used to be on the Stone Creek Road, known locally as 'Rat Abbey'.

The east fork of the lane which leads to these two farms takes us to Hill Farm which is now a builder's yard; this farm cannot have had a very long history as it was not listed in 1849. However, there was a farm close to this area, as aerial photographs show the site of the old Summergangs Farm to the south-east of the present Hill Farm buildings. There was no farm on either of these sites in the 1840/50s, so Summergangs must have been built slightly later; it was certainly shown in the 1889 OS map, Hill Farm following it, possibly at the beginning of this century.

Home Farm, on the left of the Main Road, just beyond the cemetery, was a small farm about 40 acres, and, being situated next to the Hall, it was probably, as its name suggests, used to supply produce for this establishment. However, by the 1840s this link had been severed as it then belonged to another member of the Fisher family, Mary, and was occupied by Matthew Goundrill, who held the tenancy of the farm for many years. The farmhouse and outbuildings still exist today, although most of the land has now been sold.

Until fairly recently this was the last farm on this side of the road; the two farms that we see today, namely St. Martin's and Thorn Barn Farm, are both post-war buildings. St. Martin's Farm was built in the 1960s and was part of a deal between the Hull Brewery Company Limited and the Towse family. At that time the old farmhouse was at the opposite side of the road; the Brewery, requiring a new public house close to what was then a 'new estate', converted the farmhouse into what is now the Royal Mail public house. They then built the family a new farmhouse across the road. However, the former farmhouse cannot have been very old as no building is shown on the site in 1849.

Thorn Barn Farm was just a barn and outbuildings and many people can remember it being so; the farm bungalow was not built until just after the last war. Indeed, I am informed it was the first dwelling to be built in Thorngumbald after the war when permits were still required for any building work. Part of the barn itself is of very old brick and is shown on all the old maps. This raises the question whether it is the site of the old village Tythe Barn as it is on the area occupied by the old East Field.

The first farm in the village proper, on the right hand side of the road, was Grange Farm, owned in 1850 by J. F. Butter who lived at the Hall. As no occupier is shown at the farm, he must have farmed it himself. In some earlier documents J. F. Butter is shown as a 'butcher' but the 1851 census return shows him as a farmer: maybe it was more profitable to be further back down the food chain! [In 1849 he presented a cup to Hedon Corporation, now known as the 'Buttercup'.] This farm was another to disappear in the 1960s. It was situated at what is now Beech Avenue, the entrance to the newest estate. The farmhouse itself stood back from the road but a large long barn stood alongside the main footpath; in fact, the barn was long enough to enable the Home Guard to use it as a rifle range during the last war. The lands belonging to this farm stretched through to Paull Road and the village playing field and much of the Plumtree Road estate was built on its fields. Also in this area was a large orchard and a row of plum and damson trees alongside a drain, hence the names — Plumtree and Damson Roads.

As its name suggests, Manor Farm was on the site of the old Manor House; the farmhouse was, in fact, the last of the manor houses. In the

1850s it was owned by the Mauleverer family and occupied and worked by James Wood. The farm later passed to the Johnson family who then owned the Hall; they sold it in the 1960s, again partly for housing development. The farmhouse and buildings were situated at the rear of the present amenity area and the gate posts to the farm are still there. The *Holderness Gazette* recently published an old photograph of Thorngumbald showing a gate adorned by a whalebone archway, asking its whereabouts in the village. This archway was one of the gates to Manor Farm, and Mr. Bert Billham who worked there for many years can remember digging one of the remaining stumps out in the 1930s.

Hastings Farm was owned by Robert Craven in 1849 and farmed by John Ingleby. It was another farm of about 200 acres, the farmhouse and buildings being almost opposite the present Rosedene Cottages. The last owner of this farm was Jim Turner who sold it to Mr E. Barker in the early 1960s for housing development. This was to spark the first of the building expansion which took place, and most of the land became what is now the South View Estate stretching from the Main Road to Hooks Lane and Church Lane, including Grange Road School and playing field.

During the building of Summergangs Drive, an interesting feature discovered was a spring near the farm; the builders had pumps going day and night to keep the water level down, and many of the foundations go down several feet in this area to overcome the problem.

There were several smallholdings in the village in this earlier period, most of them being 20 acres or less, but the only other large farm was on Paull Road, and at that time was called Field House Farm. It had about 70 acres, was owned by Samuel Byron and occupied by Johnathon Mitcheson. It was renamed Greenmarsh Farm in the late 1800s, a name it retains. There is an interesting feature on the front wall of the farmhouse: a benchmark is still quite clearly visible in the lower brickwork.

As you can see, many of these farms are now gone, but they live on in the names of the roads. Manor, Hastings, Grange, St. Martin's and Summergangs, all being named after local farms.

One other item associated with the village and farming was the pound, or pinfold, an enclosed area where stray animals could be penned, prior to their return to their owners (the keeper of which led to the surname, 'Pinder'). It was shown on the OS map (1855) opposite the old Manor House on the north side of the Main Road in what is now the front garden of The Homestead, a private house.

THE TRADESMEN

If farming accounted for the majority of employment in the village, what other trades and professions existed and where did the people live who followed them?

As a long, linear village, and given the fact that the common fields of the village stretched more or less the full length of the north side of the Main Road, it was natural that the south side of the Main Road became the main settlement area. There was, and still is for some of its length, a drain which runs parallel with the main road, further back known as Garth Ends Drain. This formed a natural boundary for the settlements. These garths and closes certainly existed in the 1700s, and the names of many of them can be found in land transactions and wills. West Garth, Oldhome Garth, Oxcroft Garth, Scotts Garth (still there today), Davison Garth, Stoops Garth, Old Little Close, Broome Close, Naggits Close were all of three acres or less, some only two roods.

It seems likely that for many centuries previously the village crofts and tofts would be in this area, for not only is it on high ground, so not prone to flooding, but it is also a nice sandy loam, so necessary in those days of austere living. This easily worked and productive soil which runs in a seam along both sides of the Main Road gave Thorngumbald its other main source of employment — as market gardener or nurseryman.

The 1851 census names the following gardeners: Simon Peck, George Peck, Alfred Peck, James Call, Manny Spofforth and James Elletson.

In an article on the village the *Hull News* of Saturday, 8 April, 1905, states that it is the home of the market gardener and might well be described as the 'Cottingham of Holderness'. Unfortunately, as with the farms, the market gardens have either been swallowed up in the building boom or have succumbed to the pressure put on them by the modern move to specialised glasshouse crops. Of the original nurseries only Central Nurseries, Peck's Nurseries and Scott's Garth Nursery on the Main Road still exist, although Scott's Garth Nursery has recently closed. Hook's and Fox's Nurseries, which used to be at either side of Sisters Cottages, near the shopping centre, closed a good many years ago. Peck's Nursery has a history going back to 1810 when George Peck had land in the village. The nursery today still has ties with the Peck family, the present owner's father having been brought up by them.

The other family which can boast a long tradition of craftsmanship in the village is the Willingham family. In 1845 a valuation of the village shows George Willingham as having a house, shop and garden; in 1851 the census shows his occupation as blacksmith. The Willinghams have been the village blacksmiths ever since this time, the present owner of the garage and engineering workshop being a direct descendant. The blacksmith's shop

(ALE RECOGNIZANCE.)

East-Riding of the County of York. AT a GENERAL MEETING of His Majesty's Justices of the Peace acting in and for the Division of *South Holderness* in the said Riding, held at *Hedon* in the said Riding on *Wednesday* the *eleventh* day of September, one thousand eight hundred and twenty *two* *William Roper* at the sign of the *Cross Keys* at *Thorngumbald* in the said Division, Victualler, acknowledges himself to be indebted to our Sovereign Lord the King in the sum of Thirty Pounds, and *William Ramsey* of *Hedon* in the said Riding, *Cordwainer*

acknowledges himself to be indebted to our Sovereign Lord the King in the sum of *twenty* Pounds, to be levied upon their several Goods and Chattels, Lands and Tenements, by way of Recognizance to His Majesty's use, His Heirs and Successors, UPON CONDITION that the said *William Roper* do and shall keep the true assize in uttering and selling Bread and other Victuals, Beer, Ale, and other Liquors in h *is* House; and shall not fraudulently dilute or adulterate the same, and shall not use, in uttering and selling thereof, any Pots or other Measures that are not of full size; and shall not wilfully or knowingly permit Drunkenness or Tippling, nor get drunk in h *is* House or other Premises; nor knowingly suffer any Gaming with Cards, Draughts, Dice, Bagatelle, or any other sedentary Game in h *is* House, or any of the Outhouses, Appurtenances, or Easements thereto belonging, by Journeymen, Labourers, Servants, or Apprentices; nor knowingly introduce, permit, or suffer any Bull, Bear, or Badger-baiting, Cock-fighting, or other such Sport or Amusement in any part of h *is* Premises; nor shall knowingly or designedly, and with a view to harbour and entertain such, permit or suffer Men or Women of notoriously bad fame, or dissolute Girls and Boys to assemble and meet together in h *is* House, or any of the Premises thereto belonging; nor shall keep open h *is* House, nor permit or suffer any drinking or tippling in any part of h *is* Premises, during the usual hours of Divine Service on Sundays; nor shall keep open h *is* House or other Premises during late Hours of the Night, or early in the Morning, for any other purpose than the reception of Travellers, but do keep good Rule and Order therein, according to the purport of a Licence granted for selling Ale, Beer, or other Liquors by retail, in the said House and Premises for one whole Year, commencing on the Tenth day of October next, then this Recognizance to be void, or else to remain in full force.

Taken and acknowledged before us, the day and year above-mentioned.   *Chas. Gumston.*

Chris. Sykes

Licence granted to William Roper, landlord of the Cross Keys, 1822.

[Humberside County Record Office]

was in front of the present garage on the roadside, but this was not the first blacksmith's shop in the village, for in 1849 the smithy is shown further along the road in the cottage now called Crooked Cottage. It has a large garage which stands out to the front of the row and was obviously the blacksmith's shop. The owner was Thomas Smith and it is possible that George Willingham worked for him before setting up his own business at a later date. Incidentally, Thomas Smith's apprentice in 1851 was Henry Calvert, the name of another well-known blacksmith family from Ottringham, who are also still active in the trade today.

The trade most closely linked to the blacksmith was the wheelwright's. In 1823 William Island and his son Robert provided this service at their shop at the rear of the present Post Office, which they also owned. Robert still owned the Post Office in 1887, although by then Edward Barnfather was the wheelwright and joiner, a position he filled well into the 1900s. The Post Office is still in the same position today. At one period the location was moved. At the beginning of the century Barnet Willingham, the blacksmith, took it over and moved it to the present Forge House, close to his blacksmith's shop, where it stayed until approximately 1946, when it was moved back to its original position.

There was another wheelwright in the village in 1823, John Garton, whose workshop appears to have been in the area just beyond the present garage. That was, until just after the last war, occupied by a row of houses which ran at right angles to the road and was known locally as The Rent or Teapot Row.

There were two cordwainers (shoemakers) in the village in the last century; in 1823 they were James Elletson and John Found. By 1840 James Elletson was shown as a gardener. John Found, however, appears to have been the village shoemaker until at least 1872, and there is no mention of the trade after this date, although Herbert Gardner is named as a 'boot repairer' in the early 1900s. Unfortunately, I have been unable to place any of the shoemaker's shops, although this did not altogether surprise me, as, even in my younger days, the village cobbler's shop was often only a small outside building, even a shed.

The one trade I can find no trace of is butcher (J. F. Butter's business was not in the village). The older residents can only remember being served by butchers' vans or carts from surrounding villages. None of the earlier directories lists a butcher. This, I am pleased to say, has been remedied, as we now possess one at the shopping centre.

There were several tailors in the village over the years. In 1823 there was William Jackson and by 1840 there were two: Thomas Chambers and William Richardson; by 1851, Richard Caley; and in 1872 William Dibnah. There is no further mention of a tailor in Thorngumbald. When you look at the long periods most of the other tradespeople practised in the village, it begins to look as though there was not a very good living to be made at this particular trade. The tailor's shop in the 1850s was almost certainly in the yard that is now to the rear of the Royal Mail Cottage, probably the yard where James Found had his cobbler's shop. In recent times people can remember the yard housing the village fish and chip shop; the brackets from which the sign was hung are still there at the entrance to the yard.

In 1840 builders are mentioned, with John Mitcheson given as a bricklayer, followed by Thomas Tuton in 1851; Edward Pickering was also listed as a bricklayer at this time, and in 1881 his son, John Pickering, is given as a master bricklayer employing four men and two boys. It was probably with the Pickerings that Charles Dibnah learned his trade. He went on to succeed them as the village builder in the early 1900s. It was he who built the Church Institute in 1908, on the site of the former village school that J. F. Butter had provided in 1860. There is a story that the Institute was going to be a village hall; the bricks to build it were brought from the brickyard at Hedon (until recently the pond at Locarno, Thorn Road). For this purpose they were evidently brought by the villagers on horse and cart on Sunday mornings. The Pickerings had their yard at Standidge Villas (near the old Congregational Chapel). Charlie Dibnah's house and yard were at Fir Tree House, close to the present chapel.

One interesting entry in White's 1840 *Directory* is the inclusion of Jonathon Such, a brick and tilemaker. This poses the question: did Thorngumbald have its own brickyard? There is some evidence that it did; in 1604 there is an area in the village described as Kiln Garth and the 1849 map mentions two areas, one as Brick Garth and the other as Brickyard, both suggesting that a brickmaking facility existed in the village up to this time. Maybe the bricks used in our church were produced at this kiln. There is a story handed down that the bricks used to build the church vestry were produced in the village.

After the church, some would say *before,* the next establishment which had most impact on the life of the village, I suppose, was the public house. In Thornbumgald one can be traced back to 1750, when the ale house owners had to apply at the Quarter Sessions for a licence, and some of these records still exist. In 1754/5/6 Peter Drow was Mine Host, in 1757 Anne Drow (his wife?) had taken over and held the licence until 1768. There is no record of an alehouse in Thorngumbald then until 1773 (although there is one mentioned at Ryehill — it must have been a long thirsty journey on a summer's evening). Thomas Smith held it from 1773 to 1793, then William Roper from 1822-1826, when it is called by name for the first time, The Cross Keys.

There is some confusion in the details given in directories from 1840. William Newton is mentioned as owning the Royal Mail but in 1843 William Roper owns the Black Horse and John Garton is referred to as a retailer of beer, with no pub name; I can only think he was at this time running the Royal Mail on behalf of William Newton. No mention is made again of either the Cross Keys or the Black Horse, but the 1851 census lists William Newton as living at the Royal Mail, (incidentally, he was the enumerator of this census) and he kept the Royal Mail until at least 1858.

In 1872 Misses Mary Anne and Maria Thompson were the landladies, followed by Henry Thompson in 1887. By 1897 we had another landlady, Mrs Mary Anne Rose (possibly the former Miss Mary Anne Thompson). By 1901 the village builder, Charlie Dibnah, also had the pub. Many of the older residents can remember George Wiles as the landlord in the 1920s, followed in the 1930s by Tim Barnby, Harry Marriot and Jack Stephenson. Bill Westerdale was the last landlord at the old Royal Mail which was situated on the roadside in the position that is now occupied by the front garden of the fish and chip shop and the small car park at the side. Bill took over the Royal Mail in 1942 and had the distinction of being the first landlord of the new pub when the licence was transferred. In his younger days Bill was a well-known rugby league player, playing many seasons for Hull Kingston Rovers and gaining representative honours for Yorkshire.

Not many country pub landlords could exist before the last war without some other form of income, many having other full-time jobs, other part-time jobs and small businesses. Bill Westerdale was one of the latter and ran a small scrapyard. I can still recall clearly the day Bill pulled up in his battered 'pick-up' at Salt End corner and offered me a lift home. The ride to Thorngumbald was conducted at breakneck speed, and still more disturbing was the way he managed to keep up a constant supply of cigarettes, accomplishing this by somehow driving the pick-up with his elbows while he lit one cigarette from another! On reaching the Royal Mail, he enquired, 'You alright, son?' (Everyone below the age of 50 years was 'son' to Bill.) 'Yes, thanks, thanks for the lift,' I replied, beating a hasty retreat home. Fortunately I never saw him again as I left work; for to have undergone that experience again would have been shattering.

With the demise of the trade, many of the former wheelwrights turned their hand to joinering; Tom Robinson, Jack Elletson, Mark Harrison all doubled up with this trade in the 1930s, some also acting as the village undertaker. There is an amusing anecdote told regarding Mark Harrison, who was reputedly repairing a foldyard gate for one of the local farmers when he inadvertently knocked over his box of nails into the straw. 'We'll never find them again,' angrily remarked the farmer. 'Don't worry. You'll find them all,' replied Mark. 'They will all be on your bill!'

The other occupation which had a great impact on the village was that of the 'Bobbie'. A village policeman is shown in 1881 by the name of Alfred Nicholson, a single man who lodged at one of the Sisters Cottages in Church Lane. During this century, many are remembered in the village; Albert Webster was the policeman before the First World War. He was reputedly a very lean man, which earned him the nickname of 'Whipcord Webster'. He died in August, 1916, aged 52, and is buried in the churchyard. Also recorded on the gravestone is the death of his son, killed in action in November, 1916, and another son aged 12 years died in April, 1917. What a tragic time for his family.

Police Constables Sparks, Martin, and Reardon can be remembered in the 1920s and 30s. Reardon, an Irishman, the last, lodged with a family called Northgrave who lived at the top end of The Rent. Tragically, the husband, and some time later the wife, both committed suicide in an identical manner by hanging themselves on the end of the same bed. Reardon then took up residence in one half of Leicester Cottage and was there for some years before moving on in the late 1930s. This marked the end of Thorngumbald's own police constable. From that time onwards the village was doubled up with Keyingham for policing purposes and a P.C. Hensby from Keyingham carried out this duty until well into the 1940s.

It does seem strange that at a time when the village population was fewer than 300 inhabitants, and vandalism was almost unknown, we warranted our own personal policeman, whereas in today's more troubled times, and with a population over 3,000, we have to share a police constable with half of Holderness. The most we see of a police presence in the village is a fleeting glimpse of a Panda car.

Thorngumbald Brass Band, probably early 20th century; taken in front of Burton Constable Hall.

ARSON IN THE VILLAGE

If Sir Samuel Standidge was the most famous resident of the village, the most infamous was probably Robert Billany. Below is an item from *The Calendar of Felons and Gaol Delivery, York Castle:*

On Saturday, 22 March, 1834, number 54 — age 49yrs. Robert Billany, late of Thorngumbald in the East Riding, labourer, charged upon the oaths of Peter Ingleby of the same place, farmer, and others, with strong suspicion of having on the 30th day of November last, at Thorngumbald aforesaid, maliciously and feloniously set fire to the stack of straw, the property of the said Peter Ingleby.

At the Spring Assizes Billany was found guilty and sentenced to be executed. Fortunately the story had a happier ending as the *Hull Advertiser* of Friday, 2 May, reports:

Execution at York

On Saturday last at 12 o'clock, three of the prisoners upon whom the sentence of death was passed at the late Assizes at York terminated their mortal career by the hands of the executioner, before a concourse of about six thousand spectators. The fourth, Robert Billany, who was convicted of setting fire to a stack of straw at Thorngumbald near Hull, received a reprieve on Thursday night, some doubt having arisen as to the soundness of his mind.

This was not the only case of fires reported from the village around this time. An intriguing piece of information I came across in the Humberside County Record Office, Beverley, is a notice of thanks as follows:

We the undersigned most respectfully beg leave to return our sincere thanks to our Friends and Neighbours for their kind assistance at the late FIRES at THORNGUMBALD, and more particularly to the LABOURERS for the great exertion used, and good will displayed by them on that unfortunate occasion.

Henry Cautley, John Ingleby, Thomas Straker, Jun.
Hedon, 30th Oct. 1850

These caused me many problems trying to trace exactly what the fires were, and after much searching I found the following in the *Eastern Counties Herald*, Thursday, October 24, 1850:

INCENDIARISM in HOLDERNESS

The farmers in Holderness have, during the last week, been thrown into a state of considerable excitement and alarm by the occurrence on Monday morning of three fires which broke out under such circumstances as to leave no doubt of their being the work of an incendiary, the property of Mr. Butter of Thorngumbald and Mr. Straker and Dr. Cautley, whose farms are in the vicinity of Hedon. By all these fires, a considerable degree of property has been destroyed and the suspicion of causing them has attached to a person who was formerly surgeon to the Patrington Union. He was apprehended in Hull yesterday, and we are informed is in no doubt of unsound mind. Should this be the case, it will, of course relieve the minds of owners of property in Holderness from any alarm which would naturally be occasioned to them by anything having the appearance of a commencement of a system of incendiarism, to which, happily, the neighbourhood has hitherto been, and will continue to be a stranger.

POOR HOUSES

In today's more benevolent society, it could be argued that there are no poor people, at least not in the context of the old workhouse days, but in days gone by the onus of looking after the elderly and infirm fell upon the family, in the first part, and the village when this failed.

Thorngumbald had its poor houses in the past. In 1743, Archbishop Herring's Return stated there was a poor house in the village, in which the inhabitants of the Chapelry supported two paupers. In 1757 there was also another poor house at the west end of the village. A map of 1849 shows a poor house and yard was situated just to the east of the row of white cottages in the Main Road before Willingham Garth. Thorngumbald joined Patrington Poor Law Union in 1838 and remained in it until 1935 when this was taken over by Holderness District Council, later becoming part of the responsibilities of Humberside County Council.

THE PARISH

The parish of Thorngumbald was quite distinct from the parishes of Camerton and Ryehill, until 1935, when they merged. Up to this time it had an acreage varying between 1,100 in the 17th century and 1,600 in 1858.

At the merger of 1935, Ryehill and Camerton had a total of 1,390 acres and Thorngumbald 1,657 acres. In 1971 this new parish contained 3,047 acres (1233Ha). A more recent addition to the parish is the lane known as Paull Lands Road, which, strangely enough, was always part of Paull parish until the last few years.

THE SOCIAL LIFE OF THE VILLAGE

Apart from the pub, I can find little evidence of the social life of the village. The only building remaining from the last century that has any bearing on this is what is now Ashton House, the village Reading Room in 1893, and still in use in the early 1900s, probably closing when the Church Institute was built in 1908. Reading Rooms were the forerunner of village halls, where the villagers could gather to read, play games, hold a meeting, *etc*. This house, or at least part of it, was also the Sunday School in the mid-

1800s. Ashton House is on the north side of the Main Road, nearly opposite the fish and chip shop.

THORN SHOW

Most villages had some kind of agricultural show once a year. The first I can find in Thorngumbald was held in the field known as Furdales, now occupied by Westra's Market Garden. It was not only an agricultural show but included sports and competitions, and it was also the stage for another well-known local group, the Thorngumbald Brass Band, which played at many of the villages around the area. Keyingham Foresters Friendly Society used the Brass Band many times between 1860-1891 to play at Feast Days. An entry in their records for 30 May 1860 shows £4 for Thorn Band and £14 for Patrington Band, plus 16s. 8d. for ale and grog, music and banner carriers. This band must have disbanded during the First World War, although there are people in the village who can still remember some of the instruments being around up to the last war.

The show also seems to have folded up about this time, and was not resurrected until after the Second World War, when a committee which had been formed during the war called 'Comfort for the Forces', which had been raising money to provide funds to help local servicemen, decided it would be a shame to disband, and, after much deliberation, decided to re-start the Thorngumbald Show. As there were no monies available, the 17 members all contributed £1 each to start the fund, and this was supplemented with the aid of dances, whist drives, etc., increasing the fund to £250 by the time of the first show. Thorngumbald and Ryehill Show grew in size until by the 1950s it was renowned throughout the area as one of the finest agricultural shows. In 1958, at its height, 5,000 people attended the show, the entry fee being 3s.

The show was held in the field now occupied by Summergangs Drive and Grange Road Junior School, later moving to the field behind The Crescent. Like all agricultural shows, it gradually declined in the 1960-70s, and, although it continues today, the format has changed; it is now known as Gala Day and is run by the village Gala Committee at the Junior School (back at its original site). On Gala Day the show is preceded by a procession of floats manned and decorated by the local village organisations which travel through the village ending up at the showground, still a red letter day in the village! The monies raised are used for the assistance of village organisations.

VILLAGE WELLS

The mention of the earlier shows held in the field called Furdales brings me neatly to the village wells, for it was on the roadside in front of this field that the most-used well was situated. This well, known locally as Fodlass Well (a corruption of 'Furdales'), was fronted by a fine brick wall and was shallow enough at the outside to allow horses and carts to be driven through and washed down. It was still in existence after the last war, being filled in during the 1960s. There was another well called Bellcroft Well, as the name suggests, in Bellcroft Lane, on the corner of the first left-hand bend. This was filled in during the 1970s.

The third well was not really in Thorngumbald, but in the parish of Ryehill, and was at the corner of Burstwick Road; a little of it still remains. This was called Watering Well and I have included it for two reasons: it was extensively used by the village residents in the past, and there have been recent discussions at the meetings of the Parish Council to reconstruct it.

THE SECOND WORLD WAR

The Second World War had much less impact on the village than on neighbouring Hull. The only damage from bombs I can find was a stick of incendiary bombs which was dropped across the rear of the village, from the present Junior School to Church Lane. The only war casualty was fortunately not human but a horse which was killed in a field near Thorn Villa Farm. This accident was probably caused by a stray bomb jettisoned by an enemy aircraft as it headed for the coast, a frequent occurrence for Holderness villages.

In the early part of the war the army was stationed in the village at Camerton Hall, which had been requisitioned from the owners, and also in the field that is now fronted by The Crescent. The Nissen huts which stand in front of Camerton Hall were used for the lower ranks, the Hall itself being billets for the officers, and administrative quarters. The 11th Armoured Division was stationed at both these camps and the field at the rear of The Crescent was also used at this time for tank training. The division was stationed at many villages around this area, their emblem being a black bull. When the division moved to Aldershot, the camps were used to house Italian prisoners-of-war, some of whom were transported into Hull every day and worked a three-shift system at the BOCM Mill, Foster Street. At the end of the war with Italy, and the eventual repatriation of these prisoners, the camps were used to house German prisoners-of-war, and later the homeless and sometimes countryless people of Europe who became known as 'Displaced Persons'.

Until a few years ago, the only other visible sign of the last war was the wireless station in a field between Hooks Lane and Bellcroft Lane, evidently used for aircraft, and at one time augmented by a large mobile wireless van which was situated on what is now St. Martin's Farm.

There were the usual wartime services operating for civilians. The Home Guard used the old Congregational Chapel as their headquarters. The ARP

(Air Raid Wardens) were based in the Church Institute ante-room, the siren they operated being on the Institute roof.

The War Agricultural Committee, ('War Ag' as it was generally known) also had an office in the village, based at Fir Tree House. It had far-ranging powers during the war, directing what farmers could grow and controlling all the resources of farming; it even had the powers to remove a farmer who was not farming efficiently, and sometimes did!

I would like to conclude with two items from the *Hull News* of 1905:

Last Saturday Miss Smith of Thorngumbald was severely bitten by a dog which has since been destroyed.

On Monday a serious trap accident occurred in this parish through a dog. It appears that Mrs. Gardner and her son were driving on Monday to Mr. W. Richardson's and, on turning a corner near the Church, a dog flew out at the horse causing it to shy. The occupants of the trap were both thrown out and Mrs Gardner was much hurt and her son was badly shaken.

When I read our *Village Newsletter* today, the emphasis still seems to centre on the problem of dogs in the village; it appears some things never change. Surely there are more newsworthy items than this!

Well that's it, folks! I have tried to convey a picture of what was a very small Holderness village which has suddenly become a very large one. We have no great historical distinctions, but we are today, as I suspect we always were, a friendly, caring village with lots more to do than most people realise. We *are* the largest village in Holderness, but have no wish to take Cottingham's title of the largest village in England. (Planners, please note!)

I hope as you pass through on your way to the coast, you know a little more about 'THAT VILLAGE YON SIDE OF HEDON'.

War memorial on the Church Institute, a symbol of the impact of international events on a quiet Holderness village. [Martyn Kirby]

57

BIBLIOGRAPHY

In addition to the original sources referred to in the text, the following works have been consulted:

Allison, K. J. (ed.), *A History of the County of York, East Riding Vol V Holderness, Southern Part* (1984).

Aveling, Hugh, *Post-Reformation Catholicism in East Yorkshire 1558-1790* (1960).

Crowther, Jan, *Enclosure Commissioners and Surveyors of the East Riding* (1986).

Darwent, C. E., *The Story of Fish Street Church, Hull* (1899).

English, Barbara, *The Lords of Holderness* (1979).

MacMahon, K. A. *Roads and Turnpike Trusts in Eastern Yorkshire* (1964).

Neave, David, *East Riding Friendly Societies* (1988).

Poulson, George, *History and Antiquities of the Seigniory of Holderness* (1840-1).

Sheppard, June A., *The Draining of the Marshlands of South Holderness and the Vale of York* (1966).

Smith, A. H. (ed.), *The Place Names of the East Riding of Yorkshire and York* (1937).

Smith, W. *Old Yorkshire* Vol IV (1883).

Wildridge, T. Tindall, *Old and New Hull* (1884).

Counts of Aumale

Galfrid de Gumbaud
1281

William de Gumbaud (son)
1291-1305

Margaret

Christine

Margaret
1316 = Laurence of Holbeach

Christine = Roger de Thwayt

William de Fountain
(1)
1314 = Sir Edward de Wastney (2)

Margaret
1327 = Robert de Eyville

Elizabeth Wastney
1400 = John Holme

Anne Holme
d. 1524 = William Cheyney

William Cheyney
d. 1599

Christopher Cheyney
1618

Thomas Cheyney
1633

Anne Cheyney = John Duncalfe

Jane Cheyney
1720 = John Fawsitt

John Fawsitt
1760 = Mary

1804 Mary = Robert Burton

Sarah Mauleverer
1810

Sold to J. F. Butter
1854

Elizabeth = John Turner

Joan Holme = Ralph Rokeby
1626

Laura
(1) = David of Flitwick
(2) = Thomas of Newmarket

Joan A Nun

David of Flitwick
1335

1370

Eleanor = Sir John Goodrich

Sir William Goodrich
1381

Sir Robert Goodrich

Quitclaimed to William Kelk
1394

Robert Tyrwhit
1411

Sir William Tyrwhit
1442

Sir Robert Tyrwhit
1548

Robert Tyrwhit
1591

Sold to Richard and Robert Anderson
1598

Sir William Gee
1611

Roger Gee
1757

Sold to William Scott
1776

Estate split up
1789-93

James Kay 190 acres
1793

Sir Samuel Standidge
1796

Edward Sheldon
1822

Abraham Dunn
1827

J. F. Butter
1828

WILLINGHAMS
of THORNGUMBALD
Blacksmiths and Engineers

Serving Thorngumbald and district since 1809